MANAGING
NURSERY FOOD

A PRACTICAL GUIDE FOR
EARLY YEARS PROFESSIONALS

MARY WHITING

NURSERY WORLD

A NURSERY WORLD BOOK

NURSERY WORLD

A NURSERY WORLD BOOK

First edition

First edition published in Great Britain by
TSL Education Ltd
Admiral House, 66-68 East Smithfield
London E1W 1BX

2 4 6 8 10 9 7 5 3 1

Copyright © 2001 Mary Whiting

A CIP catalogue record for this book is available from the British Library

ISBN 1-84122-015-9

Printed and bound in England by Bookcraft

Production Editor: Edward FitzGerald
Art Editor: Nicola Liddiard
Photography: Andy Crawford

Cover picture by Joy Gosney

ACKNOWLEDGEMENTS

I should like to thank the many people who have given me their time, ideas, tips and invaluable help with writing this book. In particular I should like to thank Helen Strange for her original inspiration and Barbara Crosby for her sound advice and encouragement over the years, and also Meg Knott, Stephanie Mathivet, Julie Paice, Tim Prior, Jennie Scott, Di Searle, Kristina Thompson and Julie Walker for valuable discussions on food issues in nurseries and the role of nursery managers. I am most grateful to The Caroline Walker Trust for generous permission to make use of the nutrition tables on pages 33-39. I should also like to thank Dr. Tim Lobstein at the Food Commission for his most useful comments on my early drafts and Dr. Richard Woolfson for his kind permission to quote him on page 84. In addition, I am also very indebted to Coconut Nursery, Eastside Nursery and Nunhead Nursery for sharing their delicious menu ideas.

My grateful thanks are also due to my husband who enthusiastically shopped for and cooked most of our dinners while I was writing this!

CONTENTS

INTRODUCTION

There is much concern over what British children are eating nowadays. Indeed, survey after survey show how much our children's diets have changed over the last few decades - and mostly for the worse. For example, a recent report by the Medical Research Council compared the diet of children in the 1950s with that of children today, and found that in the 1950s, children consumed more milk and red meat, and ate twice as many green vegetables, over 3 times as many eggs and $2\frac{1}{2}$ times more bread than today's children, while consumption of biscuits has risen by 4 times, confectionery by 25 times, and soft drinks by 34 times.

Overall, there has been a steady growth in the consumption of ready meals, fast-foods, sweetened manufactured drinks and snack foods which overload the digestive system with fat, salt, refined sugars and an array of additives and leave less and less room for the health-building foods that children need. We have also seen the creation of so-called 'children's food' by the food industry. The emergence of this new category of foods is a landmark change in the way we feed our children: for the first time in history, people are feeding children something different from the food they eat themselves. In addition, family mealtimes have all but disappeared in households.

All this poses serious problems for our children's health, since the foundations for good adult health are built in childhood. No amount of feasting in adulthood can make up for deficient diets in early life. The challenge for anyone in charge of feeding (especially young) children here is obvious.

This book aims to supply nursery managers with the information they need to be able to counteract these trends in their nurseries and shows, in detail, how to provide good quality, enjoyable food. It states and explains current nutritional guidelines and then describes how they can be put into practice. It also suggests solutions to a variety of situations and problems which managers may face.

1: THE RESPONSIBILITY FOR THE NURSERY'S FOOD

PROVIDING MEALS IN NURSERIES AND SCHOOLS **has often been thought of as the sole responsibility of the catering staff. Child care workers and teachers took responsibility for play and learning, but didn't consider food their 'department'. Similarly, catering staff could be defensive of their role and resent comments from another 'department'.**

To some extent, this state of affairs still remains, but rising concerns about food plus changing ideas about children's mealtimes mean that now the matter of food is not something a manager can simply leave to the caterer. After all, you, the manager, take overall responsibility for everything. In schools, teachers know that 'the Head is the school and the school is the Head'. It's the same in every kind of organisation. The personality of the person at the top, her knowledge, her abilities and her attitudes, permeates the entire workplace. In your nursery, it is largely your attitude and knowledge that can determine what the food will be like. Would you delegate responsibility for the choice of books, or the safety of the play equipment? Then neither can you with food.

The food will be better if you are seen to take a personal interest in it. You must be seen to understand the importance of a good diet and know what it comprises. You must be up-to-date on current food issues - you will get asked about them! Having a good cook is important, but you must oversee the type of food offered, how it is presented to the children, and how all meal and snack times are organised. If the manager doesn't appear to take an interest or keep herself informed, why should anyone else? Standards will slip.

WHY IS FOOD SUCH AN ISSUE?

- **Early food experiences** can set patterns for life. We've all heard people say they hate a particular food because they were once made to eat it or because they 'had it at school dinners'. Decades later, strong emotional feelings can remain. Similarly, people who grew up with sweets and chocolate bars as a part of the daily routine may well consider this normal, and pass on the habit to the next generation. Those whose families skipped breakfast may regard this important meal as superfluous and later deprive their own children of it. It can be instructive to think where one's own ideas and assumptions about food originated.

- The importance of giving children health-building and delicious food can hardly be over-estimated. Not all of your children will be fed well at home, and the nursery's contribution to these children's long term health can be significant. Nursery dinner may be some children's only proper meal that day.

Be wary of assuming that certain children 'must be' well fed at home: children from quite affluent backgrounds may be given the same narrow, fast-food diets as children from less well-off

families. Some children are fed by their *au pair*, who may have few cooking skills and may simply microwave a series of frozen meals and snacks. Where families do provide nutritious food, the nursery's role is to reinforce their good work, not undermine it. In short, whatever your children are used to at home, they need the best the nursery can provide.

• A nursery has a certain built-in authority. Parents reasonably assume the staff are professionals who know what they're doing. If some parents worry that their own food provision is not as good as they would wish, they can feel relieved that at least there are good meals at nursery. Some nurseries have built up a reputation for serving healthy and delicious food. Nowadays, many more parents are aware of healthy eating issues and expect professionals to be similarly knowledgeable. As one nursery manager told me 'Ten years ago, we were giving talks to parents about healthy eating. Nowadays it's different: parents are pretty clued up and we have to make sure that *we're* not the ones dragging behind. It is rather shaming when a parent asks "Why are you putting sugar on the apple slices?"'

The nursery's food can have a direct influence upon the children's families: you could be asked for a favourite recipe, and if you regularly have fresh fruit at snack time, children might ask for it at home. After enjoying a wedge of a fresh, sweet pineapple at nursery, one child enthused about it so much at home that her mother bought a pineapple for the first time ever. The child then explained how to cut it up, and after that, fresh pineapple became a periodic family treat. Posting up your weekly meal and snack menus can also help parents with ideas.

• Good food also benefits your staff: people have warmer feelings about a place that has good food as against one that doesn't, whilst healthy food helps to keep them fit. It can upgrade the staff's knowledge of good dietary rules and widen their horizons. It helps educate any students you may have and could influence visitors and other nearby nurseries.

• The bottom line is that anyone who undertakes to look after someone else's children has a legal duty under The 1990

Children Act to provide a healthy, balanced and varied range of meals, drinks and snacks. That duty is yours.

CHANGING EATING PATTERNS: THEIR EFFECT ON CHILDREN

There are serious health concerns resulting from

• *the gradual loss of traditional mealtimes in favour of 'grazing' and eating alone.* This results in loss of daily social interaction, plus, often, poorer quality food consumed. It is not uncommon for parents (and some child carers) to leave a child to eat alone in front of the television set while they go away to do something else, instead of eating with the child. If this happens too often it can cause various problems including food refusal. In every culture, eating is traditionally a social activity, and it appears that we eat less well if we are left to eat alone.

• *the growth in consumption of ready meals, fast-foods, sweetened manufactured drinks and snack foods.* These overload the digestive system with sugar, fat, salt, refined carbohydrates and a long list of additives; they provide little fibre and are short on a range of essential nutrients. They boost the fortunes of manufacturers as there is more profit in selling processed food than in selling raw ingredients (for example, compare the price of potatoes with that of a packet of potato crisps). But they have considerably less benefit for growing children, and store up problems for the future.

• *the creation of so-called 'children's food' by the food industry.* The emergence of this new category of foods is a landmark change in the way we feed our children: for the first time in history, people are feeding children something different from the food they eat themselves. Until now, children ate what everyone else ate. In most countries they still do. The idea of special food for babies and children is unbelievable to people of many countries.

Managers should be quite clear about this: 'children's food' is *only* an invention of the food industry. Perhaps there could be a case for special children's foods if they were exceptionally nutritious, but the ones on sale so far are nothing of the kind. Indeed, they include some of the most highly processed foods of all, and are stuffed with sugar, salt, fat and additives. Their brightly coloured labels featuring popular story-book and cartoon characters target children directly. Children see a familiar picture and want the product. This is called 'pester power' and it works like a dream. This manipulation of children's diets for the worse has serious implications for their long term health as well as creating a whole new set of problems for parents and child carers.

Nurseries can help to counteract these trends by:

• serving sit-down meals around a table, with an adult at each table, so that food can be a relaxed, sociable occasion. Children also learn how to use cutlery, about taking fair shares and other necessary skills for eating together.
• avoiding ready-made meals and fast-foods such as chips, burgers, hot-dogs, fish fingers, 'nuggets', pizzas, crisps and all other salted packet snacks, all commercial drinks (apart from unsweetened fruit juice), all confectionery, all sugary, ready-made 'desserts', and, in general, anything marketed as 'children's food'. Instead, the nursery should serve high quality food, home-cooked from fresh ingredients, which fits in with current healthy eating guidelines.

There will be some children for whom 'real' food and sit-down meals are unknown, but at least they will have the experience of them at nursery. A manager needs to know something of modern nutrition and of the dangers and deficiencies of certain types of manufactured foods, particularly including those targeted at children.

Each nursery needs a written food policy which covers the food and drink provided on all occasions and to which the same good standards apply - dinner time, snack time and tea time, plus birthdays, treats, picnics, as well as children's own cooking activities.

Other matters for a nursery manager include food hygiene, the multicultural aspect, special diets, food activities and generally marrying good practice in the kitchen with that of the playroom. There's a lot to consider, so let's go through each aspect, starting with some basic child nutrition.

2: THE ESSENTIAL CHILDHOOD NUTRITION COURSE

IT'S SIMPLE

In a way, it's very simple. If you go very light on sugar, salt, fat (particularly saturated fat) and refined white carbohydrates (food made with white flour such as white bread and white pasta) and include milk, fish, lean meat and lots of different fruit and vegetables, you can hardly go wrong. Just make sure there's plenty of variety to keep the meals interesting.

A LITTLE HISTORY

It may seem extraordinary, but many of the diseases that plague us today were largely unknown until the beginning of the twentieth century. They are still unknown in much of the world. Other diseases, caused chiefly by poverty and lack of sanitation have largely been conquered in the West, only to be replaced by a raft of new ones. These new diseases appear to be the result of extensive changes in our diet and are sometimes referred to as 'the diseases of western civilisation'. They are:

Refined carbohydrate diseases
The diseases caused by regular consumption of *refined carbohydrates* (see page 12) are many. They are thought to include tooth decay, various forms of indigestion such as gastric and duodenal ulcers, obesity, constipation and its complications of diverticulitis and haemorrhoids, appendicitis, gall stones and some urinary infections. Some of these conditions can appear quickly, even in babyhood, while others take decades to develop.

Heart disease and cancer

It is thought that these may also be linked to eating refined carbohydrates, as well as to a low consumption of fruit and vegetables. Our high consumption of fat is also considered to be a prime cause.

These conditions do not occur in countries where traditional diets are still eaten. They occur mostly in western Europe, North America and Australasia, and they begin to appear in other parts of the world whenever the traditional diet is replaced by the modern 'western' diet.

About 100 years ago, crucial changes were taking place in our food:

• *Instead of being ground by millstones, wheat was now ground by heated metal rollers, which sieved out the bran and wheat germ to produce fine white flour at low cost. Thus, for the first time in history, white flour was available to the mass of the population. It tasted good, required less chewing, and soon almost everyone was eating it.*

• *A cheap butter substitute was invented 'for the poor'. It came in blocks of fat dyed yellow to resemble butter and was named margarine. Also, as the new century progressed, farm animals were reared to be fatter. Our fat consumption soared.*

• *Sugar and salt, which had previously been either unavailable or very costly, had become commonplace and cheap.*

Gradually, new diseases began to appear. Hospitals which in Victorian times had been full of patients suffering from consumption and infections (particularly fevers and often typhoid), now struggled to deal with these new, insidious, long drawn out diseases.

It took many years for the link between the new diseases and diet, to be recognised, but it became very obvious in the UK during both World Wars, when food rationing forced the nation to eat far less sugar and fat, and when white bread was replaced by the National Wheatmeal loaf. During these war years, incidences of the new diseases fell noticeably, rising again between the wars and again afterwards when rationing stopped. It is recognised that the nation has never been healthier than during World War Two. Current healthy eating advice is very similar to that which controlled the wartime diet.

Unfortunately, we have not, as a nation, used this knowledge well. It is a profound tragedy that having conquered our old diseases, and having both the technology and the knowledge to produce first class food that could keep us fit, we have chosen instead to produce foods that make us ill.

WHAT DOES THIS MEAN FOR CHILDREN?

It means a lot. Although these diseases can take many years to incubate, they begin in childhood. Also, eating patterns established in childhood usually continue throughout life. Report after report on children's diets condemns what British children are eating. In short, they eat far too much sugar, salt, fat and not enough fruit and vegetables - the very diet that produces the whole range of 'western' diseases. Worse, it appears things are not improving. A recent report by The Medical Research Council compared the diet of children in the 1950's with what they eat today. In the 1950's, children consumed more milk and red meat, and ate twice as many green vegetables, over three times as many eggs and $2^{1/2}$ times more bread than today's children, while consumption of biscuits has risen by 4 times, confectionery by 25 times, and soft drinks by 34 times.

In 1991 a Government survey of the diets of children aged 1½–4½, found that, over a four-day period:

- *less than half ate any apples, pears or bananas*
- *only a quarter ate oranges, satsumas or any other citrus fruit*
- *less than a quarter ate any salad vegetables or raw tomatoes*
- *only a third drank any fruit juice*

BUT

- *two thirds ate sweets*
- *three quarters ate chocolate*
- *three quarters ate crisps or other salty snacks*
- *90% drank sweetened soft drinks*

The report condemned the excessive amounts of sugar and salt the children were consuming, and also the lack of essential vitamins and minerals in many children's diets.

A GUIDE TO NUTRIENTS

Water

Water is needed to replace fluids lost by breathing, urinating and sweating. Depending on how active they are, children under five lose about a litre of water a day so this must replaced, with about half coming from food and half from drinks. Plain tap water is the best thirst quencher of all.

Bottled water is not generally necessary. It may be salty, and some kinds are too high in minerals for children. To be pleasant, water should be fairly cold but should not be chilled. Children can be sick after eating or drinking something very cold, especially when they are hot.

Water should be readily available for children, especially in warm weather or when they are particularly active, to quench thirst and prevent dehydration.

Energy (calories)

Children need energy to be active and to keep warm. They also need it for their all-round growth and development, which is rapid when they are young.

All foods which contain carbohydrate, fat or protein supply energy. Fat is particularly high in energy. Under-fives need a little more fat than adults but, just as with adults, the main source of calories should be carbohydrates. The best sources of carbohydrates are cereal foods (wheat, oats, rice), root vegetables and pulses (peas, beans, lentils).

Sugar is also a form of carbohydrate; it is a rapid but short-lived source of energy which has strong disadvantages for children (see pages 13-17). It is essential for nursery managers to understand that no one 'needs sugar for energy'.

Energy is measured in kilocalories (kcals), the metric term for calories. You may also come across the term kiloJoules (kJ). 1 kcal is roughly 4.2 kJ.

Age	Average energy requirements in kcals (calories) a day
1 year	935
2 years	1,160
3 years	1,430
4 years	1,530

(Source: National Diet and Nutrition Survey: Children Aged 1$^{1}/_{2}$-4$^{1}/_{2}$ Years. Report of the Diet and Nutrition Survey. 1995. HMSO. A more detailed table, including amounts for babies, appears on page 36.)

Sugar

Not all sugars are the same. Some rot teeth and some don't. There are three types:

• **intrinsic sugar.** *This is the sugar that is chiefly found in fruit and vegetables. It is called intrinsic because the sugar is an* **intrinsic** *part of the complete food. In this form, genuinely*

WHAT ARE REFINED CARBOHYDRATES?

The term 'refined carbohydrates' usually means white flour (and therefore white bread and most cakes, buns, pies and pastries, and pasta); but it also means white rice, white semolina, and white ('pearl') barley. It also includes *extrinsic* sugars (see opposite). The term '*un*refined carbohydrates' means wholemeal flour (and therefore wholemeal bread and brown pasta), brown rice, brown semolina and brown ('pot') barley.

A grain of wheat has a paper thin outer coating called the *bran* layer which supplies fibre, quite a lot of white starch containing some nutrients called the *endosperm*, and the *germ*, which contains the richest and most varied supply of nutrients. When wheat grains are milled in the old way between millstones, the bran, germ and endosperm are all crushed together into flour and nothing is lost. The resulting flour is called 'wholewheat' or 'wholemeal' or 'unrefined'.

However, when the wheat is milled between metal rollers, the bran and wheat germ are removed leaving the white endosperm. This is called 'refined' flour. (It may then be bleached to make it look whiter).

Grains of rice which still have their outer layer are called 'brown' rice.

N.B. The bran layer is not the husk. Husks are discarded in threshing.

Most children coming to nursery will already be familiar with white, refined carbohydrates, so the nursery needs to provide regular experience of a variety of unrefined ones (see also page 17).

'natural' and unrefined, sugar does not rot teeth or encourage obesity. This is partly because it represents such a small proportion of the fruit or vegetable (a medium-sized apple, for example, contains 6-10g - about one heaped teaspoon - of table sugar), and partly because foods like fruits and vegetables are bulky and filling but not very calorific, which helps prevent obesity.

Also, because the digestive system has to process this natural sugar and turn it into blood sugar, the sugar is released gradually into the bloodstream, providing energy over a period of time.

• milk sugar. This is called lactose, and is another type of natural sugar. As with the sugar in fruit and vegetables, milk sugar is comparatively dilute, is turned gradually into blood sugar, and is harmless to children's teeth. Although referred to as milk sugar, it is also an intrinsic sugar because the lactose is an intrinsic part of the milk.

• non-milk extrinsic sugar (NME sugar). This group is quite different. Here we are talking about sugar which was in food (such as in sugar beet or sugar cane) but which has been extracted, hence 'extrinsic'. It is what most people think of as sugar. It can be white or brown and includes granulated, caster, icing, demerara, soft brown and muscovado sugar as well as syrup, treacle and molasses. In commercial products it is often referred to as 'added' sugar.

It's found in a huge range of foods - cakes, biscuits, breakfast cereals, pastries, jam, sweets, chocolate, concentrated fruit juices and spreads, soft drinks, ice-cream... and in a wide range of savoury foods including baked beans, meat pies, cheese spread, bottled and cook-in sauces and paté. It can appear liberally in foods marketed as 'healthy' such as muesli and cereal bars. On food labels, words ending with '-ose' such as *dextrose, glucose, sucrose, fructose* and *maltose* simply mean 'sugar'. Some foods contain several different types of extrinsic sugar. It is essential to read labels when shopping.

Extrinsic sugar is the type that rots teeth. Babies' and children's teeth are particularly vulnerable. One of the most distressing things that can happen to a young child is to have to go to the dentist to have a tooth (or teeth) drilled or extracted. Other problems also arise here over fear of needles and risks with anaesthetics. Sometimes, and horrifically, babies' teeth have to be extracted because they are erupting already black with decay.

All this is completely avoidable. Anyone who cares for children should be very aware of the appalling state of British children's teeth because of excessive sugar consumption. After some years of improvement, the situation is now worsening. A recent survey by The Mancunian Community Health NHS Trust found that nearly half the three year olds in Manchester suffered from tooth decay, and more than half of those had rampant decay in more than five teeth.

As a nation, we pay lip service to the matter, but carry on much as before. People who try to limit their children's consumption of sweets can easily find themselves accused of being 'cruel'!

Tooth decay closely parallels the amount, and, most importantly, the *frequency*, of (extrinsic) sugar consumed.

The most damaging way for children to have a sugary food or drink is on its own as a snack. If it's eaten or drunk along with other foods as part of a meal, the effect of sugar is lessened. Antacid foods such as milk and cheese have a cleansing effect on teeth and make a good finish to a meal which contained sugar.

DO CHILDREN NEED SUGAR FOR ENERGY?

The amount of energy we have depends on the amount of sugar in our bloodstream - 'blood sugar'. Our bodies can make blood sugar from every kind of food we eat, but most easily from carbohydrate foods. The food is processed bit by bit as we eat it and turned into blood sugar, which we then use up, quickly or slowly, depending on what we're doing. Insulin, made by the pancreas, regulates the amount of sugar in our blood - if there's too much, it removes some and stores it in the liver as glycogen. Larger surpluses get stored as fat - our body's way, evolutionarily-learned, of dealing with any future shortage, when the fat can be turned back into blood sugar.

If our blood sugar level is high we feel energetic; if it's low, we don't. Blood sugar also affects mood. With too little, we can feel cross or irritable; with more we tend to feel more cheerful.

However, eating extrinsic sugar upsets this process. Refined sugar needs little further processing by the body so whizzes into the bloodstream in three to four seconds (blood sugar made by eating bread takes about four minutes), bumping the blood sugar levels right up. But then insulin rushes in to remove the surplus, causing a drop in blood sugar. Thus eating sugar provides a quick, but unsustained, burst of energy, and can contribute to mood swings. There is good anecdotal evidence of children becoming 'high' on sugar, with resulting behavioural problems.

In summary:

- *energy is obtained from every kind of food, particularly carbohydrates*

- *sugar is not a good source: its effect is short lived and it causes other problems.*

What about honey?

Many people think of honey as a natural food and therefore good for us. Well, it *is* a natural food - but only for bees. As human food, it behaves like other types of refined sugar, and will rot teeth just as badly. Actually, it is *slightly* less harmful than table sugar and does contain small quantities of nutrients, so in a straight choice between honey and sugar, honey wins - but only just.

And what about sugar in drinks?

Most soft drinks and squashes contain sugar. Some contain sugar and artificial sweeteners as well. Although such drinks don't stick on to teeth as food can, they are still a hazard, especially for front teeth which are washed over by the sugar solution. In addition, they are usually acidic. The acid attacks tooth enamel and wears it away. All types of such drinks should be avoided at nursery.

Drinks containing artificial sweeteners instead of (or as well as) sugar should also be avoided, as these sweeteners are something of an unknown quantity. The acids put into such drinks will still put teeth at risk.

Fresh fruit juice sounds like a healthy option, but it is also acidic, and once a fruit has been squeezed, its juice presents the same risk to teeth as other sweet drinks. Very diluted fruit juice can be offered with meals but at other times plain water and milk are safer for teeth. (See page 117).

In summary:

- *avoid bottled, canned and packet drinks of all kinds.*

- *pure squeezed fruit juice, well diluted, is a possible drink at mealtimes.*

- *milk and plain water are the best drinks, especially between meals.*

Sweet expectations

One of the problems of giving sugared food to children is that they quickly become accustomed to the taste and reject anything less sweet. This can set up long- term preferences that can be difficult to change. (See also Chapter 9 on babies and sugar)

DIETARY FIBRE

First please read page 12. Sometimes called roughage, cellulose or unavailable carbohydrate, this is a strange nutrient because it is not absorbed. However, it is crucial for bulking out food, thus keeping the intestines healthy and preventing constipation and its complications. Fibre can be soluble or non-soluble but the best source for preventing constipation is the bran contained in wholewheat flour. Brown rice is a good source as are many fruits and vegetables, particularly peaches, strawberries, apricots, plums, all pulses, parsnips, sweetcorn and plantains.

When changing to a more wholegrain diet:

• *a gradual change over a few weeks is essential to give the digestive system time to adapt. Otherwise children could suffer from a period of discomfort and diarrhoea.*

• *for the same reason, bran should not be added to food. Nor should bran- or fibre-enriched cereals be given. Children don't need fibre in such concentration. Added bran can make their food too bulky and leave them short of calories. It can also absorb and remove nutrients.*

Nurseries should provide wholegrain foods and dishes containing plenty of fruit and vegetables. Laxatives should not be needed when the diet contains enough fibre.

PROTEIN

Protein is needed for general growth and maintenance of the body. Children need proportionally more protein than adults.

Babies proportionally need about two to three times as much! Nearly all British children (99%) get enough protein, in common with most other children in the Western world.

Protein is obtained from animal sources such as meat, fish, eggs and milk, but can also be obtained from plant sources such as pulses (including tofu), and cereal foods. (See page 117 on protein and vegetarians.)

FAT

Some fats in our body transport nutrients in the bloodstream, and some fats are used to make brain cells and others cells. However, fat is chiefly used as a source of energy as it is very calorie-dense. Unused calories are stored as layers of fat in the body. The idea is to consume and use the same number of calories in order to keep fit and avoid becoming too thin or too fat.

It is recommended that adults and children over five should get no more than 35% of their calories from fat, but as a nation we eat far more than this.

There are no exact recommendations for the amount of fat for under-fives. A breast-fed baby gets 50% of its energy from fat, and it is accepted that under-two's need a fair amount of fat and that, for example, they should be given full fat milk and not skimmed or semi-skimmed. The general opinion is that between babyhood and the age of five the proportion of energy obtained from fat should gradually fall to 35%.

CALCIUM

There is more calcium in our bodies than any other mineral. It has many functions, but is needed most importantly for building bones and teeth. Of all the calcium in our body:

- *98% is in our bones.*

What are saturated and unsaturated fats?

Saturated fats Animal fats (meat fat, butter and cream) are the most highly saturated fats. Palm oil and coconut fat are also saturated - though less so than animal fat. Saturated fats are usually solid at room temperature. They are chemically 'rigid' fats; they pose health problems when eaten in quantity, and are considered to contribute to heart disease and cancer. At present our national diet is too high in saturated fat.

Unsaturated fats These are liquid at room temperature and include most plant oils - sunflower oil, corn oil, safflower oil, and so on. Fish oils are also unsaturated. We are advised to substitute unsaturated fats for saturated ones.

Monounsaturated fats Olive oil, rape-seed oil and avocado pears contain monounsaturated fat, which is considered to be the healthiest option, although research into the health benefits of olive oil continues.

Sometimes liquid plant oils are treated with hydrogen to harden them so they can be used in food products such as margarine, biscuits, cakes, ready meals and so on. This *hydrogenation* removes some, or all, of their health benefits by changing unsaturated fat into saturated fat. The process also creates *transfats*, which are not much found in natural fats and which are considered a possible problem. Some recent research suggests that hydrogenated fats are the most damaging of all.

Most children under five get plenty of saturated fat as cream in their milk. This is fine for this age group, but a nursery needs to provide unsaturated fats, particularly fish oils, rather than too many more saturated fats (see also page 20).

- *1% is in our teeth.*

- *1% is in soft tissues, and does many jobs including regulating heart beat and helping the blood to clot.*

Our bones are constantly being 'remodelled': replacing old bone with new. A child's skeleton is completely replaced about

Are fish oils especially good?

Yes! They are rich in what are called *omega-3* oils or *essential fatty acids*. They are essential for the proper development of the brain and blood vessels. We need these oils at every stage of our lives, but developing embryos, babies and young children have a particular need. There is interesting new research linking various current health problems, notably depression and heart disease, with our falling fish consumption.

Oily fish rather than white fish are particularly rich in these essential oils. Herring, sardines and mackerel are best, but pilchards, salmon, trout, sprats and tuna (fresh rather than tinned) are all good.

The nursery should serve oily fish regularly and in ways that children will enjoy.

Note that nuts and seeds, such as sunflower and sesame seeds and tahini, can be alternatives to oily fish, but see the warning on pages 118-119.

every two years. In order to avoid osteoporosis in later life, it's important to build up strong bones right from childhood. Milk is probably the best source of calcium for children and is rich in many other nutrients. It is hard to get enough calcium without milk, and most children under five get about half their calcium from milk. Whole milk should be given to the under-two's and a mixture of semi-skimmed and whole milk to the two-to-five's, depending on what else individual children are eating. Skimmed milk is not suitable for children under five.

Children who don't have milk or milk products need to get good supplies of calcium from other sources (see page 33). About one child in ten doesn't get enough calcium.

IRON

Iron was one of the first minerals to be studied, and we now know a lot about its great importance. All children need plenty of iron because they are growing and therefore constantly making more blood. Iron is essential for doing this.

However, most British children don't get enough iron. Many surveys over the years have reported this deficiency, and at the moment it is estimated that 84% of children get less than the recommended amount and 16% of children get very little. When children (or adults) are short of iron they become *anaemic*. They then lack energy, are prone to infections and may look pale. They may also find it harder to learn, have a short attention span and become forgetful. When diet is poor, this can continue for years, thus affecting children's education as well as their health. However, symptoms of anaemia are not always obvious, so prevention is crucial.

A little iron is found in most unprocessed foods because all cells have iron as part of their internal structure, but growing children need to have good sources of iron daily.

There are two kinds of iron in food:

• *haem iron which is found in meat, especially kidney and liver (but see pages 24-25), meat products, egg yolks and some fish such as sardines and pilchards. Haem iron is easily absorbed into the bloodstream so haem iron-rich foods are particularly useful.*

• *non-haem iron which is found in plants such as apricots, wheat germ, wholewheat bread and cereals, pulses (peas, beans and lentils), dried fruit and dark green leafy vegetables. A form of non-haem iron is added to some breakfast cereals and bread.*

Non-haem iron is less well absorbed. For example, some of the iron in leafy vegetables is held in insoluble compounds which renders it unavailable. In a mixed diet, only about half the iron eaten gets absorbed. It's not the total amount of iron in any food

Was Popeye wrong?

Let's debunk the oft-quoted myth that 'children must have spinach'. It can be a surprise to learn that spinach isn't the exceptional source of iron it was once believed to be:

• *the amount of iron was overestimated tenfold because a researcher put the decimal point in the wrong place - and thereafter this was the figure always quoted!*
• *although spinach contains a lot of iron, at least half of it is bound up by the presence of oxalic acid, making it impossible to absorb. (Similarly, the calcium in spinach is not well absorbed for the same reason.)*
• *in any case, children often find it difficult to eat spinach in any quantity. Some hate it because of its strong flavour and the way it sets their teeth on edge. As there is no way it can be forced upon them (nor should it be - see pages 82-84), it remains of minimal practical use in a nursery.*

that matters, but how much of it can be absorbed. In general, the softer the texture of any food, the more of its iron gets used.

Absorbing iron

Iron absorption is increased when it is eaten in the same meal as a vitamin C-rich food. One excellent idea is to give a glass of diluted orange juice, or slices of an orange or kiwi fruit with a meal containing iron-rich food.

The refining of flour and other cereals is claimed to be a major cause of anaemia. Wholegrain flour is rich in iron, white flour is not, so by law, white bread must be 'enriched' by the addition of a form of iron (finely ground iron filings). However, the amount is much smaller than in wholewheat, and there is also debate over how well this form of iron is absorbed. Some breakfast cereals are also 'enriched' or 'fortified' with iron (see pages 27-28).

In the 1995 *National Diet and Nutrition Survey: Children aged 1½-4½ Years*, the chief sources of non-haem iron were found to be 'fortified' cereals and cereal products, such was the low consumption of other iron-rich food. This survey found that children in this age group ate very little meat and got only 5% of their iron from haem sources. In the 1950's children ate more iron from such sources as red meat.

ZINC

It's worth mentioning zinc because marginal deficiencies can occur in children when they are going through a big growth spurt. All tissues in the body contain zinc, and it is essential in the body's use of protein, carbohydrates and fat. A deficiency can cause retarded growth, some skin conditions, and slow healing of wounds and burns. It is estimated that 72% of British children get less than the recommended amount, with 14% of children going very short.

Like iron, zinc is best obtained from animal sources: liver, red meat and eggs. Shellfish are a superb source, especially oysters. Wholegrain bread, wholegrain pasta and pulses (peas, beans, lentils) are other good sources.

BORON, COBALT, COPPER, IODINE, MAGNESIUM, MANGANESE, POTASSIUM, SELENIUM, ETC.

These are some of the other minerals essential for body maintenance and general good health. Although very small amounts are needed, deficiencies can sometimes occur. Food grown on fertile soil and without the use of chemical fertilizers tends to be richer in these (and other) nutrients. *Selenium* is a good example of this. There is less selenium in our bread than previously partly because Britain no longer imports selenium-rich Canadian wheat. British wheat has less selenium because our soil is low in it.

Children should eat a wide range of good foods, in order to get enough of these minerals. Such foods include meat, eggs, fish, milk, milk products, wholegrain cereals (wholewheat flour, bread and pasta; wholegrain breakfast cereals), and a variety of fruit and vegetables.

SALT (SODIUM CHLORIDE)

It is generally recognised that in this country we eat too much salt, which leads to serious health problems such as high blood pressure, strokes and osteoporosis. Although these conditions do not affect children, the habit of eating over-salted food can easily be acquired in childhood and then remain. Unlike sweetness, salt is an acquired taste. Children who have not been given salted food will not miss it. Generally speaking, the more salt people get used to, the more they will crave.

Babies under one year old should not be given salted food at all: their kidneys are not fully developed and cannot do their usual job of ridding the body of excess salt. The salt then accumulates and can cause harm, even death. Children between the ages of one and five should still be given very little salt. Beware of ready made, composite foods, and tins and packets of savoury foods which can be heavily salted. One UK survey discovered that only 10% of our salt consumption came from the natural salt content of foods; 15% was added in cooking or at the table, and 75% came from ready-prepared foods. Salt is a tasty spice, but a dangerous one.

VITAMIN A (RETINOL AND CAROTENE)

Children need good quantities of vitamin A, more than adults in fact, because it is so important for growth. It is also needed for good eyesight and it helps fight infections by boosting the immune system. It is thought to have a role in preventing cancer and heart disease. There are two types:

• *retinol, from animal foods: fish liver oils (e.g. cod liver oil), fish, meat, whole milk, cheese, eggs, butter. By law, margarine must have retinol added; this is also added to some other spreads.*

Since the mid-seventies, farm animals have had vitamin A added to their feed. The surplus accumulates in their livers, with the result that lambs', calves' and pigs' liver now contain over *twice* the vitamin A they did before. Chicken and ox livers also contain much more than before. Therefore, liver should not be given more than once a week as large amounts are toxic.

• *carotene from brightly-coloured fruit and vegetables such as carrots, tomatoes, peppers, mangoes, apricots and dark green leafy vegetables. Carotene is converted into retinol by the body, although it takes six units of carotene to make one unit of retinol. However, it is thought that carotene has other properties which protect against cancer and heart disease.*

Carotene isn't toxic, although eating very large quantities of carotene-rich foods can turn the skin a yellowish orange colour.

The 1995 *National Survey of Children aged 1½-4½* found that 44% of children were getting less than the recommended amount of vitamin A, and 8% were getting very little. It is recommended therefore that all children under five should be given vitamin drops containing vitamin A.

VITAMIN DROPS

It is recommended by the Department of Health that all children under five should be given vitamin drops containing vitamin A, C and D. It is important that no *extra* drops or other vitamin A supplements are given because too much can be toxic. Vitamins A and D are fat soluble which means any surplus accumulates in the body.

Families who receive Income Support or income-based Jobseekers Allowance can get free vitamin drops. A family's GP or Health Visitor can give more information.

VITAMIN B

There is a whole family of B vitamins, sometimes referred to as the 'vitamin B complex'. Each individual B vitamin has a name and a number, and they work together *synergistically*. They are found in every cell of the body and are needed by every cell. This

means that if there is a deficiency, every cell in the body will suffer, and symptoms can be wide ranging. Antibiotics destroy B vitamins. In some countries, children who are given antibiotics are also given a prescription for a vitamin B supplement.

In general, they are essential for the good development of the brain and nervous system and a variety of other bodily processes. They dissolve in water, which means any surplus is discarded in the urine and not stored. Therefore foods rich in vitamin B need to be eaten every day. The best sources of the group as a whole are liver, wheat germ, wholegrain breads, wholegrain pasta and yoghurt.

Some of the B vitamins are worth looking at individually:

Folate (folic acid)
Because it was originally discovered in green leafy vegetables - foliage - the name 'folate' was invented. It is particularly important in early pregnancy for the development of the foetus and the prevention of spina bifida. It is thought that children probably get enough folate, although assessment is difficult. Deficiency can lead to a type of anaemia.

Vitamin B 6
This has many functions such as aiding the normal functioning of the brain. Deficiency can cause eczema and anaemia, and psychological conditions such as nervousness and irritability, but deficiency is rare when a good, varied diet is eaten. It works closely with vitamin B12.

Vitamin B 12
This naturally occurs only in meat and other animal foods. It is added to 'fortified' breakfast cereals, some yeast extracts and 'fortified' blackcurrant drinks. It is important for those feeding vegan children to ensure that their intake of B12 is satisfactory. For other children there is no problem.

FORTIFIED JUNK

British laws on food 'fortification' are extremely lax, and manufacturers are allowed to add almost any nutrient they wish to their products. Most 'fortified' or 'enriched' products are of low nutritional quality, high in added sugar, salt or fat. In plain language they are no more than fortified junk. Worse, such products are often aimed directly at children by the use of brightly-coloured packaging depicting cartoon and familiar story-book characters.

A recent report by the Food Commission on fortified foods (see page 131) found that 83% of the products aimed at children were high in either sugar, salt or fat. Several breakfast cereals containing over one third sugar were in child-enticing packets, including one which boasted of '8 vitamins plus iron'. Another cereal, labelled 'fortified with vitamins' was over half (56%) sugar, making it one of the sugariest cereals ever sold. Some iced biscuits claimed to be 'a nutritious snack', 'developed by nutritionists', even though their chief ingredient was sugar. Rather than solving the problem of modern children's diets, such foods add to it. This kind of 'fortification' is not allowed elsewhere in Europe, and it is hoped that new EU legislation will eventually control the situation here.

As it is, the nutritional claims play on parents' anxieties and confuse them about what nutritious food actually is. In fact, the extra nutrients are of limited value. Not only are they normally present in very small amounts - often the minimum allowed to make the nutrition claim - but the ones most commonly added are unneeded by most people in the UK. Childhood deficiencies in vitamin C or calcium, for example, are rare. Also, a nutrient taken out of its natural context is less beneficial. For instance, the anti-oxidant potential of vitamin C is only 15%, the rest coming from secondary plant substances. There is therefore no comparison between a soft drink with added vitamin C and real orange juice. Also, some nutrients, such as vitamins A and D, folate and several minerals, have narrower safety margins, and in a virtually unregulated system there is a potential for overdosing, producing a metabolic imbalance or toxicity. (This did occur years ago, fatally, when infant formula, cereal and cod liver oil were fortified.)

Fortified breakfast cereals do make a contribution to the intake of B vitamins and (in girls) iron, with children of low nutritional status, although part of the benefit may come from the milk consumed with the cereal.

Nursery policy should be to ignore all health claims and buy only food which is valid on its own merits. Good food needs no 'fortification'.

Fortification's honourable intentions

The practice of food fortification started in 1925 when manufacturers voluntarily added vitamins A and D to margarine. In 1940, when butter was in short supply, the practice was made compulsory on the grounds that margarine was being used extensively instead of butter and should have a similar nutritional value. The requirements still apply to margarine but not to lower fat spreads, although many manufacturers add them voluntarily.

Also in 1940, calcium carbonate (chalk) had to be added to white flour, and later iron and thiamin (B1) and niacin (B3) were added. These requirements still stand. The addition of iodine to salt was also introduced to prevent goitre.

Only the folic acid (folate) campaign, introduced to reduce the incidence of spina bifida, may get government approval, but the issue is contentious. At present, some manufacturers add folic acid to a range of foods.

VITAMIN C

This is probably the best known vitamin of all. Most people know that it's essential and that it's found in oranges. Most people also know that a deficiency causes scurvy.

Vitamin C, scurvy and sailors

Scurvy is a fatal disease. Mild scurvy lowers resistance to infections, reduces energy and makes skin bruise and gums bleed easily. Prolonged lack of vitamin C gradually creates more and more problems since it is needed by every cell in the body, and if untreated, eventually leads to death.

Scurvy was once common, particularly amongst sailors who had no fresh produce on their long voyages. When Captain Cook made his crew collect and eat greenstuff at every possible opportunity, there was, remarkably, no scurvy. Later, British sailors were given limes to keep them well, thus gaining the nickname 'limeys'. But although such practices continued successfully for 200 years, no one knew *why* greenstuff and lime juice prevented scurvy. Vitamin C wasn't isolated and named until 1934.

In fact, there's hardly a function in the body that doesn't involve vitamin C . It is essential for healthy skin, teeth, gums and blood vessels and for wound healing. It fights off infections, helps control blood cholesterol and aids iron absorption. It's a prime anti-oxidant and is thought to help prevent cancer.

It is found in all fresh fruits and vegetables, especially in oranges, blackcurrants, strawberries, peppers, tomatoes, kiwi fruit, green leafy vegetables - and, surprisingly, in tinned guava. Because it is water soluble and cannot be stored in the body, vitamin C-rich foods must be eaten every day.

Vitamin C is fragile and is easily lost by:

- *storage*

- *heat, such as in cooking and keeping food warm*

- *leaching out into cooking water, such as when boiling vegetables*

- *oxygen attacking the cut surfaces of chopped up food*

One of the reasons that we are all advised to eat 'five-a-day' helpings of fruit and vegetables is to ensure a high intake of protective vitamin C.

VITAMIN D

Vitamin D is essential if children are to have good bones and teeth. Particularly between the ages of six months and three years, children's bodies are making new bone very rapidly. If their bones are going to be strong then plenty of vitamin D is needed. Calcium cannot be absorbed without it. It is also necessary for general, all round normal growth and development. It is fat soluble and therefore, as with vitamin A, the body can store it.

Vitamin D maintains the right levels of calcium and phosphorus in the blood. Long term deficiency causes *rickets*, resulting in malformed bones such as bowed legs, knock-knees and being pigeon-chested. Babies may have bulging foreheads. There may also be muscle weakness and painful muscle spasms *(tetany)*. In addition, children suffering from vitamin D deficiency tend to be lethargic and morose.

Rickets is thankfully rare in Britain today, but partial deficiency is more common. Bones and teeth that were partially deprived of vitamin D in early childhood may show smaller malformations.

Unlike other nutrients, the best source of this vitamin is not a food at all, but sunlight. The ultraviolet (UV) radiation in sunshine makes vitamin D directly on the natural oils on exposed skin. Even in a comparatively cool country like Britain, summer sunshine is our best source for everyone over the age of three. Asian children living in Britain sometimes suffer from Vitamin D deficiency, possibly because of less exposure to sunlight. It is a matter of concern that, having banished rickets from this country a few decades ago, we are now allowing it to creep back, possibly because children are now being kept indoors more.

There is plenty of UV in summer, less in spring and autumn and none in winter, so the nursery should aim for children to be outdoors for part of each day in summertime. Of course, hot sun should be avoided as it can cause sunburn and skin cancer, so nurseries must arrange for shaded outdoor play areas and suitable clothing.

This presents something of a dilemma: if children are kept out of direct sunlight, and/or wear cover-up clothing in summer, and/or wear sun-block creams, they will be protected from sunburn and skin cancer, but might not be able to absorb enough vitamin D. No one really knows the answer to this, but all are agreed that urgent research is needed. This is little practical help to anyone caring for young children, who have to make some kind of provision for sun safety. Arrangements should be made for such things as cotton sun hats and shaded play areas for hot days, but also for some exposure on 'cloudy-bright' days.

A few foods supply vitamin D. Oily fish is the best source, but margarine, some other spreads and some breakfast cereals have vitamin D added. There is also some vitamin D in eggs and liver. Because of concern that young children may not be getting enough of this vitamin, vitamin drops are recommended for under fives (see page 25).

VITAMIN E

Curiously perhaps, although vitamin E is needed by every cell in the body, it seems to have only one function. That is to prevent oxygen destroying vitamin A and other nutrients, particularly *essential fatty acids*. After fulfilling this task, the vitamin itself is used up or destroyed. Destruction of nutrients by oxygen is called *oxidation*. A small excess of Vitamin E can be stored in the body but is quickly used up. Toxicity from Vitamin E is unknown apart from experimental, massive dosages.

ANTI-OXIDANTS

It may seem strange that something so essential to life as oxygen can also destroy substances that are also essential to life, but there it is. When oxygen destroys nutrients, this is called *oxidation*. There are three vitamins which fight oxidation in the body: vitamins A, C and E, sometimes referred to as the *anti-oxidant* or *ACE* vitamins. It is thought that anti-oxidants protect against cancer and heart disease.

The ACE vitamins are found in a whole range of fruits and vegetables, particularly strongly coloured ones. It is one of the reasons we are advised to eat plenty of fruit and vegetables every day.

It is recommended that all children and adults eat at least five portions of fruit and vegetables every day, excluding potatoes. One (diluted) pure, unsugared fruit juice drink can count as a portion. In terms of weight, it means roughly 200g (6-7 ounces) in all, for a child aged 4-5 per day. More is excellent.

The wheat germ in wholemeal flour is rich in vitamin E, but since Britain went over to eating bread made from refined white flour in which all the vitamin E is destroyed, our consumption has fallen dramatically. Some people think this alone could account for the rise in heart disease this century. Amongst a wide range of other benefits, vitamin E is said to aid recovery from heart attacks.

A nursery which regularly provides green coloured plants, non-skimmed milk and non-skimmed milk products, and bread and pasta made from wholewheat flour, should be providing its children with enough of this vitamin.

VITAMIN K

Although present in a number of foods, such as egg yolk, cheese and wholemeal flour, and especially in broccoli, enough vitamin

SOURCES OF VITAMINS AND MINERALS

Nutrient	Why/good sources	Average daily need for a child aged 2–4 years
Water	To replace water lost in breathing sweating and urinating. Water, fruit, vegetables, salads, soups, and all drinks.	About 1 litre with about half coming from drinks.
Energy (calories)	To replace used energy. All foods, including fat, carbohydrates (starch and sugar), and protein.	1130–1600 kcal 4720–6730kJ
Starch (complex carbohydrate)	For energy. Bread, flour, cereals, pasta, rice, potatoes, root vegetables, pulses.	About 150–250g
Fibre (roughage)	For the smooth running of the digestive system and preventing constipation and related diseases. Wholemeal bread, flour and pasta, wholegrain cereals, brown rice, beans, peas, and lentils, root vegetables, potatoes, plantain, some fruits including, apricots, peaches, strawberries and other berries and dried fruit.	10–15g
Added sugar (extrinsic sugar)	No nutritional need: enough sugar is obtained from many foods, and surpluses are stored as fat. Cakes, sweets, biscuits, most drinks, puddings, chocolate, most breakfast cereals, jam, jelly, ice cream, sweetened yoghurts etc.	Nil
Protein	For building muscle and blood cells and general growth and maintenance. Meat, fish, cheese, milk, eggs, pulses, tofu, seeds, nuts, cereals, bread, rice.	15–19g
Fats and oils	For energy; for carrying nutrients around the body; for making cells, including brain cells; surpluses are stored as fat. Full-cream milk, cream, butter, cheese; margarine, cooking fats; oils, fish, meat, nuts, meat products, eggs, pastry, cake, suet, chocolate, ice cream, biscuits, chips, crisps.	40–60g
Calcium	For building good bones and teeth. Milk, cheese, yoghurt, tofu, sardines, pilchards, leafy vegetables, soya fortified with calcium, cheese spread, tinned salmon, pulses, sesame seeds and tahini, white flour and bread, dried fruit, oranges, egg yolk.	400–450mg
Iron	For making blood and preventing anaemia. Liver (especially pork liver), kidney, liver sausage and paté, fortified breakfast cereals, red meat, wholemeal flour and bread, 'wheatbiscs', corned beef, sardines, pilchards, soy beans, chick peas, lentils, dark green leafy vegetables, dried apricots, raisins, baked beans, salmon, tuna, herrings, eggs.	6–7 mg

SOURCES OF VITAMINS AND MINERALS continued

Nutrient	Why/good sources	Average daily need for a child aged 2–4 years
Other minerals (zinc, selenium, copper, magnesium, etc)	Various essential jobs involving growth, repair and maintenance. As with iron, animal sources, where available, are absorbed better.	Various small amounts.
Salt	Very tiny amounts only are needed to help with water balance. Many foods; salt is added commercially to bread, soup, processed meats, pies and sausages, and ready-made sauces, spreads, snacks and meals of all kinds.	Up to 50g, which is easily got from salt occurring naturally in food. No more is needed.
Vitamin A	For good eyesight and night vision; essential for normal growth and maintenance; fights infection by boosting the immune system; is an anti-oxidant. Liver, fish liver oils, carrots, spinach, sweet potatoes, red peppers, mangoes, apricots (dried, tinned and fresh), nectarines, peaches, tomatoes, broccoli, margarine, butter, cheese, kidney.	400–500ug (or 5 vitamin drops plus a normal diet.)
Vitamin B family	Crucial for the development of the brain and nervous system; for all round growth, healthy skin, digestion, for the release of energy and other vital functions. Liver, kidney, meat, yoghurt, milk, cheese, tinned fish, nuts, seeds, brown rice, fortified breakfast cereals, leafy vegetables.	Various small amounts.
Vitamin B1 (thiamin)	For normal growth, good appetite and digestion and maintaining the nervous system; for the release of energy. Yeast, liver, wheat germ, wholemeal bread, flour and cereals, lean pork, ham and bacon, sunflower seeds, brown rice.	Small amounts.
Vitamin B2 (riboflavin)	Essential for growth; for healthy eyes and digestion; regulates the thyroid gland. Milk, yoghurt, cheese, kidney, liver, egg yolk, red meat, wheat germ, wholemeal bread and cereals, green leafy vegetables. Sunlight destroys B2, so when milk is left in the sunshine, B2 is lost.	Small amounts.
Vitamin B3 (niacin)	For controlling the release of energy from food; for appetite and digestion. Kidney, liver, red meat, poultry, brown rice, bread, sunflower seeds, tinned fish (especially tuna), fortified breakfast cereals.	Small amounts.

SOURCES OF VITAMINS AND MINERALS continued

Nutrient	Why/good sources	Average daily need for a child aged 2–4 years
Folate (folic acid)	For making and maintaining red and white blood cells. Liver, kidney, green leafy vegetables, wholemeal flour and bread, eggs, pulses, avocado pears, bananas and oranges.	70–100ug.
Vitamin B12	Needed by every cell in the body for normal functioning, especially red blood cells and in the nervous system; works closely with B6 and folate; prevents pernicious anaemia. It is only found in animal foods: meat, oily fish, cheese, milk and eggs. It is added to a few other foods such as fortified breakfast cereals, fortified blackcurrant (and some other) drinks and some yeast extracts.	
Vitamin B6 (pyridoxine)	For using protein to build new tissues; for making antibodies and red blood cells. Liver, pork, red meat, fish, wheat germ, wholemeal bread and flour, fortified breakfast cereals, bananas, various vegetables.	Small amounts.
Vitamin C	Needed by every cell in the body, it has numerous functions; fights infections, helps healing of wounds and fractures; essential in making collagen needed for building bones, teeth, tendons and skin; an anti-oxidant, thus helping fight cancer and heart disease; helps the body to absorb and use iron. All fresh fruits and vegetables, especially oranges, raw blackcurrants, strawberries, raw red and green peppers, spring greens, broccoli, cabbage, cauliflower, spinach, tomato, kiwi fruit, mango, grapefruit, potatoes.	30 mg at least; many British children get too little.
Vitamin D	Works with calcium to build bones and teeth Sunlight on the skin, oily fish (sardines, tuna, pilchards, salmon), cod liver oil, margarines and spreads, eggs, butter, fortified breakfast cereals.	Small amounts; some deficiencies, chiefly amongst Asian children.
Vitamin E	For preventing oxidation (destruction) of vitamin A and essential fatty acids, thus helping prevent cancer and heart disease; needed by every cell in the body. Wheat germ, wholemeal bread and flour and wholegrain cereals, nuts and seeds, seed oils (eg sunflower, safflower, grape seed), green coloured plants, milk, egg yolk.	Small amounts.

K can be made by any healthy person in the intestine. Antibiotics destroy vitamin K, but yoghurt increases the number of healthy intestinal bacteria. (See also page 26.)

The figures in the following tables were compiled by the Department of Health Committee on Medical Aspects of Food and Nutrition Policy (COMA) 1995. The tables themselves are reproduced from 'Eating well for Under Fives in Child Care' by kind permission of The Caroline Walker Trust.

When using the tables, it should be noted that:

- *some children will need more, some less. It depends on*
  - *the metabolism and body size of the individual child*
  - *in the case of calories, on how active a child is*
- *children's appetites vary from day to day, and menus vary from day to day. Therefore, it is sensible to average these figures out over a week or so.*

HOW MANY CALORIES DO UNDER-FIVES NEED?

ESTIMATED AVERAGE REQUIREMENT FOR ENERGY PER DAY FOR UNDER-FIVES		
Age of child	Boys	Girls
6 months	760 kcal (3,200kJ)	710 kcal (2,980kJ)
9 months	880 kcal (3,680kJ)	820 kcal (3,420kJ)
1 year	960 kcal (4,020kJ)	910 kcal (3,800kJ)
1½ years	1,080 kcal (4,520kJ)	1,020 kcal (4,260kJ)
2 years	1,190 kcal (4,960kJ)	1,130 kcal (4,720kJ)
2½ years	1,280 kcal (5,370kJ)	1,230 kcal (5,140kJ)
3 years	1,490 kcal (6,230kJ)	1,370 kcal (5,730kJ)
4 years	1,600 kcal (6,730kJ)	1,460 kcal (6,120kJ)
5 years	1,720 kcal (7,190kJ)	1,550 kcal (6,480kJ)

It is interesting to compare these figures with those for adults (HMSO figures):

Age	Men	Women
20–50 years	2,550 kcal	1,940 kcal

By age five, boys' daily need for calories is already over two-thirds of the amount they'll need each day as adults, and girls' daily need is already almost three-quarters of their daily adult need.

FOOD AND EXERCISE

Very active children will obviously need more calories than less active children. By eating more food to replenish the spent calories, children will also be consuming more other nutrients too. A less active child who doesn't need to replace so many calories will probably be eating less food - and thus getting fewer nutrients all round.

It is difficult for an inactive child to get enough nutrients for proper growth and development, so it's important for children to be active for a good part of each day.

WHERE SHOULD THE CALORIES COME FROM?
HOW MANY FROM FAT?
HOW MANY FROM CARBOHYDRATE FOODS?

There are no precise guidelines for children under five. However, it is accepted that:

• *children under two need considerably more fat than adults.*

• *children over five need the same amount as adults.*

• *children between the ages of two and five need a moderate amount of fat. This is needed for good growth and development and to supply fat-soluble nutrients. It is accepted that after the age of two, the amount of fat in children's diets should gradually decrease until they are about five, when it should reach the adult level.*

Official recommendations for sources of energy for adults and children over five:

• *50% of energy (calories) should come from carbohydrates, and of this: starch, milk sugar and intrinsic sugars should make up **at least** 39%; extrinsic sugar (NME sugar) should make up 11% **at most.***

• *35% **or less** of energy should come from fats but **no more than** 11% of this must be from saturated fats.*

• *15% of energy will come from protein.*

HOW MUCH PROTEIN DO UNDER-FIVES NEED?

Age of child	Grams per day
7–9 months	13.7
10–12 months	14.9
1–3 years	14.5
4–6 years	19.7

HOW MUCH OF WHICH VITAMINS DO UNDER-FIVES NEED?

These are the current recommendations for daily amounts of some important vitamins.

Vitamin	7–9 months	10–12 months	1–3 years	4–6 years
B1 (thiamin) mg per day	0.2	0.3	0.5	0.7
B2 (riboflavin) mg per day	0.4	0.4	0.6	0.8
B3 (niacin) mg per day	4	5	8	11
B6 (pyridoxine) mg per day	0.3	0.4	0.7	0.7
B12 ug per day	0.4	0.4	0.5	0.8
Folate ug per day	50	50	70	100
A ug per day	350	350	500	500
C mg per day	25	25	30	100
D ug per day	7	7	7	no specification

HOW MUCH OF WHICH MINERALS FOR UNDER-FIVES?

These are the current recommendations for daily amounts of some important minerals.

Minerals	7–9 months	10–12 months	1–3 years	4–6 years
Calcium mg per day	525	525	350	450
Iron mg per day	7.8	7.8	6.9	6.1
Zinc mg per day	5.0	5.0	5.0	6.5
Potassium mg per day	700	700	800	1100
Magnesium mg per day	75	80	85	120
Selenium mg per day	10	10	15	20
Iodine mg per day	60	60	70	100

PERCENTAGES OF CHILDREN IN BRITAIN AGED 1¹/₂ – 4¹/₂ WHO ARE GETTING LESS THAN THE RECOMMENDED AMOUNT OF CERTAIN NUTRIENTS	
Vitamin A	44
Vitamin B6	8
Folate	6
Vitamin C	38
Iron	84
Calcium	11
Zinc	72

Figures are from *The National Diet and Nutrition Survey: Children aged 1¹/₂ – 4¹/₂ Years.* 1995.

ADDITIVES

The subject of additives causes much concern and debate. On the one hand, governments and food manufacturers assure us that all additives in British food have been rigorously tested and are perfectly safe. On the other, many of such additives are banned in baby foods, and from time to time an additive that has been used for many years is withdrawn. Some additives are banned in this country but allowed, for example, in the USA - and vice versa. Colourings are not allowed by law in foods made for babies, but are allowed in other foods widely eaten by children: such foods as dessert toppings, ice lollies, sausages and squash are not sold as 'specially for babies and young children' and so may legally contain the full range of additives.

Most additives are concerned with making food seem more attractive than it would be without the range of flavour enhancers, texturisers, emulsifiers, acidifiers, bulking agents, gelling agents, anti-caking agents and so on. They can disguise off-colours and off-flavours. They can make watery stuff look thick and make food seem fresh even when it is months old.

Concern has been expressed over the sheer quantity of additives that now go into ready prepared foods. (One researcher worked out that by the age of eighteen, children could have eaten their own body weight in additives!) A child who eats several commercial food items in a meal could receive large amounts of some additives, and in an unpredictable and unresearched combination. No one has ever researched what is called 'the cocktail effect': consuming mixtures of additives from different products.

Because of their smaller body size and less developed immune systems, young children are especially vulnerable to adverse effects. The best advice is to avoid ready prepared foods, apart from actual 'baby' foods which are protected by law - although even these use refined starches (now with E numbers) with dubious effects, such as fermentation problems, on the digestive tract. Some additives seem to cause particular problems to children with allergies, and some have been linked to behavioural problems. Good quality food doesn't need additives.

ADDITIVES TO AVOID	
There are possible problems with these additives:	
Colours	**Preservatives**
E102 tartrazine	Benzoates: E210-E219
E104 quinoline yellow	Sulphites: E220-E224, E226-7
E110 sunset yellow	
E122 carmoisine	
E123 amaranth	
E124 ponceau	
E127 erythrosine	**Anti-oxidants**
128 red 2G	Gallates: E310-E312
E131 patent blue	E320 (BHA), E321 (BHT)
E132 indigo carmine	
133 brilliant blue	
E151 black PN	
154 brown FK	
155 chocolate brown HT	**Sweeteners and flavour enhancers**
E160b solvent-extracted annatto	Monosodium glutomate: 621
E161g canthaxanthin	Saccharin
E180 pigment rubine	Aspartame

3: SO WHAT WILL YOU SERVE?

A GOOD KNOWLEDGE OF NUTRITION is essential, but how are you going to put it into practice? Let's summarise some of the information in Chapter Two and see how your nursery can use it.

British children are eating too much: sugar, salt, fat and refined white starch; too many processed foods; and possibly too many additives.

British children are consuming vast quantities of sweets and chocolate bars, soft drinks, highly sugared breakfast cereals, biscuits, crisps and other salted packet snacks, chips, burgers, sausages, sugary and salty tinned foods, mass produced factory white bread and other white flour bakery goods, and all kinds of salty, additive-laden 'novelty' foods and desserts.

For some children, foods such as these form the basis of their diet.

Children are not eating enough: fresh fruits and vegetables, wholemeal bread and other wholegrain foods; nutrient-packed foods such as liver, kidney, lean red meat, fish and egg yolk. Many children are getting less than the recommended amounts of certain nutrients, especially calcium and iron (see table on page 40).

Few British children eat diets that are based on these highly nutritious foods. Such foods as wholemeal bread and fresh fish are unknown to many children. Overall, children are missing out on freshly prepared, home-made food made from nutritious ingredients.

This situation has to be taken seriously because such poor diet leads directly to future health problems such as tooth decay, appendicitis, obesity, strokes, heart disease, some cancers, osteoporosis and constipation with its many complications including diverticulosis. Tooth decay and appendicitis can affect even the youngest child, while the other conditions take several decades to incubate. Early eating patterns are crucial since they often determine adult ones.

SUGAR

Added sugar is nutritionally unnecessary and should be avoided as much as possible. It rots teeth and can cause behavioural problems. UK children's consumption of sugar is colossal, and much of it is the form of sweets and other sugary snack foods. Unsurprisingly, our children's teeth are the worst in Europe. A recent food industry survey stated that:

- *£1.9 billion of confectionery is consumed by children every year*

- *20% of all confectionery is consumed by the age of eight*

- *children eat 34% of all confectionery sold*

- *only 5% of that is bought by children themselves. **Adults buy the remaining 29% for them***

Between-meal snacks cause the most damage to teeth. However, children who don't eat sweets but like sugary food at mealtimes, such as having sugar on already-sugared breakfast cereals, are also risking decayed teeth. Sugary food can also lead to over-consumption of calories and obesity.

Nursery policy
Cook the food yourselves or issue firm guidelines to caterers. Closely inspect the labels of all tins, packets and anything ready made. Look out for the '-ose' words: fructose, glucose, maltose, dextrose and so on, which all mean SUGAR. Watch out for sugar in savoury foods too. Also look out for other forms of sugar: honey, syrup, molasses, concentrated fruit juice or spreads, jam, jelly, and so on. Some products contain four or five different forms of sugar! Such foods have no place in a nursery.

Professional child carers should not make children more liable for drillings and extractions.

Aim to serve no more than *one* food a day with sugar in it - if that - and keep sugar strictly for mealtimes when its damaging effect is lessened. Avoid confectionery and also all snacks and drinks which contain sugar in any of the forms mentioned above. Serve fruit or cheese at the end of a meal, and hunt for interesting variations on this: for example, serve ripe pears with cheese as a delicious meal ending (a traditional Italian one), or have cheese and grapes or apple slices. Collect dessert recipes made with fruit and minimal (or no) sugar. In the case of cooked puddings, reduce the amount of sugar by at least a third - they will taste the same! Make sure any sugared puddings have distinct nutritional advantages: fruit crumbles, banana custard, milk puddings and fruit bread contain sugar but also have plentiful nutrients. Serve pieces of cheese after a sweet pudding because cheese has a cleansing effect on teeth.

DON'T WORRY, THEY'LL CLEAN THEIR TEETH AFTERWARDS!

How often one hears this! But anyone who has watched children cleaning their teeth will know what a poor job many of them make of it, and anyway, toothbrush bristles can't get into every nook and cranny where sugar can hide. Moreover, sugar begins to work on teeth soon after it hits them and reaches its peak of activity within minutes. Most of the damage will be done before the toothbrush is even picked up. Of course children need to learn about tooth brushing from an early age so it becomes an automatic good habit, but don't think that it will somehow magically undo all the damage done by eating sugar. It won't.

Bottled drinks. These tend to be acidic (look for 'citric acid' on the label). When an acidic drink or food has been taken, the resulting acidity of the mouth makes tooth surfaces vulnerable for a while afterwards. In this acidic environment, scrubbing teeth will do more harm than good. Cheese is a good meal ending and will help restore the mouth's natural acidity level.

If you serve breakfast, avoid sugary breakfast cereals and *never* allow sugar to be sprinkled on cereal (see on page 65). For snacks, make fresh fruit the rule - or pieces of raw vegetable if children enjoy this as a change. If you think children need more than that with their milk, serve chunks of good bread, which they can enjoy breaking up with their fingers, and perhaps eat with thin curls of cheese.

Avoid using confectionery as a 'treat' or reward. Apart from the necessity of making decisions about what exactly deserves a sweet and what doesn't, and it can become competitive and create hurt feelings.

Also, it's not fair to lead children to expect a sweet (or any other present) because they have done something well. What they should be able to expect, is fair recognition, and frequent, appropriate, warm praise. If you want to give something tangible on birthdays or 'to make your bumped knee better', give a little paper sticker, with a quickly drawn smiley face or a sun (or something of the child's choice) on it, and put it on the child's jumper. More personal, longer lasting than a sweet and highly visible! It's also cheaper, and can create good feeling between the child and the adult who made the sticker.

BIRTHDAYS

• Children's birthdays should be celebrated in some way at nursery, but don't have to involve food at all. Different nurseries have different ideas, including (usually) singing a happy-birthday song and giving four big 'birthday claps' to the new four year-old. In addition, the birthday child might use a long taper to light four big candles on a pretend birthday cake and then blow them out (very exciting!), or sit on a special chair or cushion, wear a Birthday Hat, or have their name attached to a big balloon fixed in a prominent place, or have a privilege like helping an adult with a certain special job.

There is absolutely no need to put on any kind of 'birthday tea', attempt party games or anything of that kind. Not all children will enjoy this sudden change of routine (including possibly the birthday child), and in any case using the time for play is more beneficial.

• Occasionally, a parent may want to bring in a cake, or even chocolate bars and fizzy drinks 'so the nursery can give a party'. Of course, you don't have to agree to this. It can so easily become competitive, and various practical problems arise. The food may not fit in with the nursery's agreed food policy, as well as being unsuitable in some other way such as having an unmentioned allergenic ingredient that could make someone ill. There are additional problems with grease from creamy cakes and the colourings and stickiness in sweets and spilled drinks. In letting parents bring their own free choice of 'party food', the nursery loses control over what the children are eating, while still being responsible for it. It's up to parents to celebrate their children's birthdays at home in the way they wish, and at nursery, the nursery takes responsibility of what to do.

The nursery needs a 'birthday policy'. Write it out and post it up. Draw coloured balloons around it or whatever to make it prominent. State that your nursery celebrates all its children's birthdays, and say, briefly, how you do it. Say you don't have parties as such because children benefit more by keeping to a familiar routine and having more time for play. You could invite parents to their children's candle-lighting ceremony, however, and say what time that will be - first thing in the morning could be easiest. Mention the subject when you talk to new parents, and write it in your Parents' Welcome Pack. (And see page 69.)

If, however, a parent really wants to bring something, you could suggest that she bring a little fresh fruit for the children to eat as an extra treat at snack time. If word gets around that you are accepting fresh fruit for birthdays, that's fine - the nursery may receive more!

SALT

Adding salt to young children's food is nutritionally unnecessary as children get all the salt they need from the numerous foods which naturally contain salt. Salt interferes with calcium absorption and can lead to high blood pressure and strokes.

Unfortunately, salt is added to many ready made foods, sometimes in large quantities (most bread is very salty for example). More salt may be added in cooking and at the table. The salty taste is attractive - and the more that is eaten the more may be wanted. However, unlike sweetness, saltiness is an acquired taste. Unsalted children's food tastes bland to us only because we have become used to having salt in almost everything.

Nursery policy

Keep salt consumption down to a bare minimum. If children are not used to salty-tasting food they won't miss it. Particularly avoid having salted packet snacks: salt can be sprayed directly onto these, so the salty taste is immediate and strong, accustoming children's taste buds to the flavour. Such snacks have no place in a nursery.

Potatoes, rice, pasta and vegetables should be cooked without salt. Save the unsalted but tasty water from cooking vegetables (except cabbage, Brussels sprouts or broccoli cooking water which is not suitable) for the next day's vegetables to give extra flavour. It can also be used in stews and soups as vegetable stock. In recipes, add bay leaves, onion, carrot, thyme, sage, fresh parsley and so on to give a good flavour.

When ordering food, simply don't order obviously salty food like sausages, burgers, pies and ready-made fillings and sauces. Buy, for example, only low-sugar, low-salt baked beans.

FAT

Our national high consumption of fat has been strongly linked to our high rate of heart disease. Saturated fats - in meat and poultry fat, butter, palm oil, coconut fat and artificially hardened (hydrogenated) oils - are the problem, and children should get no more than about 10% of their energy from saturated fat. However, the mono- and polyunsaturated fats in oily fish, seed oils and olive oil (and goose fat!) are different and beneficial. In all, children should get no more than 30-35% of their energy from fats and oils.

Ready-made foods can often be high in saturated fat. If you have ever eaten unsalted crisps, you will know how greasy they taste when the grease is undisguised by salt. Fried foods, especially deep fried foods such as chips, samosas and spring rolls, soak up large amounts of fat and should be largely avoided.

Nursery policy

When ordering food, forget about ready-made foods such as burgers, pies, biscuits, frozen chips, packet snacks, sausages and children's 'novelty' dinners. They're all fatty, including vegetarian ones. (Perhaps a local butcher could make you up a batch of low-salt, low-fat sausages?) Red meat is nutritious and a useful source of iron, but make sure all the fat is cut off before cooking, and that the gravy is well-skimmed (fat separator jugs do this job brilliantly and are cheap). Skim chicken gravy well, too. Don't order suet or hard cooking fats. A *little* butter may be needed for a particular - and occasional - recipe, but use a sunflower margarine labelled as 'high in polyunsaturates' as a spread.

Use olive oil and seed oils in cooking. Give children a regular taste of sardines, fresh mackerel, salmon, trout, tuna and pilchards from an early age. Even a very small portion, perhaps eaten on toast or with mashed potato or with a good sauce can teach children that fish is delicious.

Remember that children need more fat than adults, so don't give them some kind of adult slimming diet! They need Cheddar not cottage cheese, semi-skimmed not skimmed milk, creamy not low-fat yoghurt, and so on, or they could go short on calories.

REFINED WHITE STARCH

This means white flour and anything made with it: bread, pasta, biscuits, pies, cakes. It also means white rice and white semolina. It causes constipation which can lead to many serious complications over the years. Wholemeal flour products help prevent constipation and contain a wide range of nutrients.

Nursery policy

Serve a mixture of breads, but always have wholemeal. Standard wholemeal sliced bread can be less than delicious, so try to get something locally baked with a better flavour (check for the addition of nuts and seeds - see pages 118-119). Wholemeal pitta bread is often popular. Serve different kinds of pasta: white, wholewheat and spinach. Brown rice pudding is something a bit different and delicious.

In the kitchen, sometimes use wholemeal flour and sometimes 81% extraction flour (also called 'wheatmeal' or 'brown'), which is finely sieved wholemeal, and roughly half-way between wholemeal and white. 81% extraction flour can be used in all cooking.

PROCESSED FOODS

Processing destroys a range of nutrients, so processed foods generally tend to be of low nutritional value. They are also frequently high in sugar, salt and fat, low in fibre and may have a long list of additives. Some boast of having 'added vitamins' but such additions do not compensate for the overall losses (and see pages 27-28).

Nursery policy
You don't need them. Stick to fresh food.

FRUIT AND VEGETABLES

All adults and children are recommended to have five portions a day, to obtain a wide range of nutrients.

Nursery policy
Have fruit and/or vegetable sticks available along with milk for the mid morning snack; offer at least two vegetables and one fruit at dinner time; serve more fruit or vegetables at tea time.

FIVE A DAY!

There are no recommendations for the size of a 'portion' for under fives, although the adult 'portion' is set at 100g (3-4 oz), giving half a kilo (1¼ lbs) a day. Some children will be able to eat a small banana or half an apple and should be encouraged to do so. Build a range of fruit and vegetables into your menus and recipes, so children will become accustomed to them. Because cooked vegetables are more concentrated than raw ones (they lose water in cooking) and need less chewing, more may get eaten. However, some children prefer raw vegetables to cooked ones, so make use of both kinds. Some ideas for your menus:

A helping of:
Home-made tomato sauce
Bubble-and-squeak (with Brussels sprouts, cabbage or broccoli)
Puréed vegetable soup
Carrots mashed with swede, with butter and black pepper
Tinned sweetcorn (in water)
Cooked peas, broccoli, sweet potatoes, beetroot, cauliflower, peppers, aubergine
Ratatouille
Raw red & yellow peppers, carrots, vine tomatoes, watercress, cauliflower, broccoli

Fruit pie or crumble, or stewed/tinned fruit
A cup of diluted orange juice or cloudy apple juice
A few orange segments
A satsuma or clementine
A kiwi fruit
Half a peach, pear, apple or nectarine
A small banana, perhaps in banana custard
(raisins, sultanas & currants are useful but lack vitamin C)

Any raw fruit in season! Try sweet pineapples and pink melons and watermelon cut into wedges or chunks, plums (stoned), blackberries and red summer fruits.

Salads take up a lot of stomach space and are more useful to slimmers than to growing children. Keep them on the menu, but serve just a little as an accompaniment to something more nutrient-dense.

FREE FRUIT FOR NURSERIES!

There is an EU scheme whereby nurseries, schools, hospitals, registered charities and other such institutions can gain access to surplus fruit and vegetables. For more information, contact The Intervention Board's Fruit and Vegetables Withdrawals Section on 0118 953 1694/1913, or fax 0118 953 1261. Ask for the information sheet called *Free Distribution of Withdrawn Fruit and Vegetables* and for form HOR 17 (charities), HOR 18 (schools), or HOR 19 (institutions).

Note, however, that the minimum amount allowed is a pallet weighing about 750 kilos. In the case of fruit, a pallet is about 50 boxes and typically contains 5,000 to 6,000 pieces of fruit! Also, the fruit you apply for must be *in addition* to your normal catering order. Of course, the produce could be given out for children to take home. Nurseries may get together (perhaps joining with nearby schools) and make a joint application. Supply depends on the market, and you may get only one or two day's notice that fruit will be available. But worth looking into. Also, look out for the promised Government-funded free-fruit scheme.

THE BEST USE OF THE BEST FOODS

It is crucial that your food tastes good or it won't be eaten. It should be served neither too hot nor too cold, be of pleasant and varied texture and *look* inviting. Make it a priority to find delicious ways of cooking the most nutritious foods so children will get to like them. If the liver is hard and dry, or the fish is overcooked to a smelly mush (both well-known in institutions), children will reject it, and why shouldn't they?

Try different ways of cooking and presenting foods until you find one that your particular children like. Below are some delicious ideas for liver, kidney, fish, eggs, milk, carrots, tomatoes, broccoli, Brussels sprouts and fresh fruit.

LIVER

The more you cook it the tougher and nastier it gets. Cook it super-slowly until it has *just* stopped being pink in the middle. Disguise its dry taste with sweet vegetables such as tiny peas, well stewed-down onion, potatoes mashed with creamy milk, and ratatouille. Try these extra ideas:

Spaghetti sauce: stew plenty of chopped onion in olive oil until soft and lightly coloured. Stir in roughly chopped up chicken livers and toss over medium heat for 3-4 minutes. Stir in some wholewheat flour and toss again. Add stock or vegetable cooking water, tinned tomatoes, a good squirt of tomato ketchup, some thyme and basil. Simmer, stirring occasionally and mashing down the livers with a potato masher. After half an hour or so you should have a thickened, tasty sauce. The livers will have 'disappeared'. Optionally, add sliced mushrooms with the stock. Serve with wholewheat pasta, grated cheese and a green salad.

Dinosaur stew: (first, train your butcher to cut liver for you in *thin* slices. It's easier to slice when the meat is semi-frozen.) Stew plenty of sliced onions in olive oil until soft and yellow. Meanwhile, cut the slices into triangles and other odd shapes (dinosaur bits!), then toss in wholewheat flour and a little mustard powder. Stew the liver slices very slowly on top of the cooked onions until *just* done. Remove the liver to a serving plate. Pour in enough stock and milk to make a sauce, stir up, let it bubble for a minute then pour over the liver pieces. Serve with peas and mashed potatoes.

Make your own chicken liver paté, using fried onion, garlic, parsley and a dab of real butter. Serve with hot toast with lettuce and tomato.

KIDNEY

Steak and kidney stew is the obvious choice. Use the two meats 50-50. Use plenty of onions, a little carrot and good stock to give it flavour. Cook it as slowly as possible for as long as possible until the meat can be cut with a wooden spoon. To increase the treat, make it into a pie (top crust only) with thinly rolled out home-made pastry. Serve with carrots, and green beans or peas. Optionally, add mushroom slices.

Make a wonderful Lancashire hot-pot with kidney, mutton or lamb, onions, mushrooms and potatoes.

OILY FISH

Serve sardines on shredded lettuce on hot toast. In winter, fry them in a speck of olive oil to warm them first.

Serve a Portuguese salad: sardines with a salad of avocado and

tomato pieces and thin cucumber slices, along with crusty white bread.

Serve slightly warmed pilchards with mashed potato and salad.

Mackerel in apricot sauce: grill fresh mackerel, fillet, then serve flakes of the delicious flesh in apricot sauce; stew chopped onion in olive oil until soft. Stir in a little ground cumin, cook for a minute, then mix in puréed apricots tinned in syrup. (Yes, it's a very sweet sauce, but it's scrumptious and makes the best introduction I know to mackerel.)

Make pink fish cakes with tinned salmon, mashed potato and a dash of ketchup.

Serve cooked, flaked white fish, tuna or salmon with spinach pasta and mushroom slices.

Make fish paste: beat tinned fish into curd or cream cheese with lemon juice. Serve on toast.

WHITE FISH (COD, PLAICE, WHITING, COLEY, HADDOCK, ETC)

Steam over boiling water, very slowly until *just* done, i.e. until the fish can be broken into flakes with a fork. Serve with mashed potato, and a home-made white sauce containing pan-browned mushroom slices, chopped fresh parsley or grated Cheddar.

Make a good tomato sauce (see page 61) and serve with fish, along with rice or pasta.

Make into little fish cakes with mashed potato and fresh, chopped parsley. Serve with oven chips and tomato sauce.

Pack a fish cake mixture into a fish mould and turn out.

EGGS

Serve them scrambled on toast. You can make them smoother by adding a little arrowroot or cornflour slaked in water. Cook at the last moment.

Chop hard-boiled, cooled eggs into a little mayonnaise and serve on bread with lettuce and/or watercress.

Golden eggs: mix tomato purée and ketchup into the above mixtures.

Serve pieces of hard-boiled egg as finger food; serve quarters of scotch eggs.

Chop hot, hard-boiled eggs with a little sunflower margarine into jacket potatoes, perhaps with chopped cooked bacon.

Add to salads; add cooked pieces to composite dishes such as lasagne, broccoli cheese (see below), fish pie and moussaka.

Add to milk shakes (see below), and whisk into sauces.

MILK

Serve milk sauces (cheese, mushroom, parsley) with fish as above and also with chicken. Try mushroom sauce with chopped ham in it with chicken - terrific. Try onion sauce (lots of finely chopped, cooked onion in white sauce) with lamb.

Whisk powdered milk generously into milk sauces to add extra calcium and to make them seem creamier.

Make macaroni cheese with lots of home-made cheese sauce. Serve with sautéed potatoes, bacon bits and roast tomato slices. Use in cauliflower/broccoli cheese (as below).

Use evaporated milk – which is simply milk that has been boiled and evaporated (don't confuse it with sweetened, condensed milk). Use instead of custard; stir into porridge and milk puddings; serve as an alternative to milk with cereals.

Serve milk puddings. Serve (white or brown) rice pudding: use only a little sugar, add lots of sultanas, a little vanilla and a grating of nutmeg. If semolina is stirred all the time it won't go lumpy; serve it with stewed fruit.

Serve 'nursery hot *café crème*', a good drink in cold weather: warm milk (never over-heated or the flavour will be ruined) with a few grains of coffee stirred in.

Milk shakes: liquidise semi-skimmed milk with powdered milk, plain yoghurt, vanilla, nutmeg and fruit. Very ripe bananas are excellent. Perhaps add hard-boiled egg. Almost a meal!

Serve home-made quiches: roll the home-made pastry very thin, and cover the base with chopped cooked onion for a specially good flavour. Cheese-and-bacon is a favourite filling but try others, such as tomato-and-spinach, tuna-and-sweetcorn, or broccoli/cauliflower-and-bacon. Always scatter grated cheese over the top for a golden topping. Serve with mashed potato and a green leafy vegetable, green beans or a salad.

Serve fruit egg-custards: make the same as for quiches (omitting the onion!). Add a little sugar and plenty of cooked, drained peaches, nectarines, plums, apricots, or fresh strawberries or blueberries.

Remember that full fat yoghurt has all the qualities of whole milk but is easier to digest and that the calcium is better absorbed. Buy (or make) plain yoghurt and sweeten it with orange juice and fruit – not with sugar. Make luscious yoghurt-fruit desserts. Children can stir in their own fruit at the table.

Remember other milk products: serve a variety of cheeses (don't buy 'low fat' versions); serve home made cheesecakes with added sultanas, mixed spice and grated lemon rind; try to find smatana and serve it with fruit.

SMATANA

Smatana, like yoghurt, is a traditional fermented milk product. It is a delicious food and tastes something like a mixture of yoghurt, crème fraiche and sour cream, and can be used as a substitute for any of these (and also for fresh cream) in many recipes. It has 10% fat. It is available from supermarkets and some delicatessens, although some parts of the country are bereft of it.

CARROTS

At dinner time, serve a 'red mountain': mix puréed, cooked carrot with a little mashed potato, a dab of butter and black pepper. Pile it up spectacularly, and surround with parsley sprigs or a broccoli/Brussels sprout purée (see below) for 'grass'. Children can eat pieces of the mountain!

Serve raw carrots, topped, tailed, peeled (unless organic), and cut into sticks, matchsticks, chunks, slices, diagonal slices and so on. Vary the shape each time. You might occasionally offer dips (hummus, cream cheese beaten with milk and chives, taramasalata, mayonnaise) if this gets more carrot (and other raw vegetables) eaten.

Serve cooked carrots cut as above. When they're *just* cooked and not soft and pulpy, toss in a little sunflower margarine or a tiny dab of real butter, and, to make them taste sweeter and fresher, plenty of chopped, fresh parsley.

Serve them along with other vegetables, chopped or sliced finely, in curries, pasta sauces, lasagne, pilaffs, moussaka or mixed vegetable bakes under cheese sauce.

__Roasted carrots:__ toss (1cm) diced carrots in olive oil, then roast at gas 6 (200°C) for about 40 minutes, or until soft and slightly browned. Toss two or three times during cooking. Sometimes mix with diced parsnips, swede, beetroot or sweet potato.

BROCCOLI

__Break into florets__ and boil uncovered until bright green and *just* done. Don't overcook it or keep it warm or it will go limp and grey and smell bad. Arrange as little 'trees' on a bed of mashed potato or rice. Cook cauliflower florets the same way. Perhaps mix the two in the same 'forest'.

Cook as above. Put into a serving dish, cover with a good home-made cheese sauce. Cover the top with extra grated cheese mixed with breadcrumbs and a dusting of paprika. Grill for a moment to make the top an appetising, crunchy, golden brown. Treat cauliflower the same way and mix the two together. Be generous with the sauce – it's the means of 'selling' the veg!

As above, but with bits of crumbled, grilled bacon mixed in. Sometimes make a mix of vegetables: add pieces of cooked potato and carrot or baby tomatoes.

Cook as above and purée with a little mashed potato, a lump of butter and a pinch of pepper to make a 'green mountain'. Pile it up high and let children eat the mountain. Surround with parsley sprigs for 'grass'. (Perhaps turn it into a volcano with tomato slices piled on the top!)

Boil little florets until bright green - a few minutes only, then put into a sieve, hold under the cold tap to set the bright green colour, then serve as crudités for a snack. The brief boiling softens them a little and makes them easier to chew and swallow.

Make bubble-and-squeak, as with Brussels sprouts, below.

Make broccoli 'lily pads': cut thin slices off very fat broccoli stalks, the more irregularly shaped stalks the better. Steam or boil them briefly, then serve either as finger food at snack time, or as a vegetable at lunch time.

BRUSSELS SPROUTS

Boil uncovered until *just* cooked, not until soft and squashy. Avoid keeping warm. At the last moment, toss in a dab of real butter, a tiny squeeze of lemon juice and a grinding of black pepper. This will kill the bitter taste. Serve them as 'baby cabbages' growing in a 'field' of mashed potato.

Purée them and make a 'green mountain' as with broccoli, above. Make a similar mountain with green cabbage.

Cut them raw into thin sticks, and serve in salads or as crudités. Don't call them Brussels sprouts if you think the name will be off putting.

Bubble-and-squeak: chop or mash cooked sprouts into a little mashed potato. Shape into patties, and fry in a little bacon fat mixed with olive oil until the undersides are golden brown. Brown the other side. Traditionally served with bacon and grilled tomatoes, but you can serve it with any meat. Good with tomato sauce. Also make it with cabbage, Brussels tops, mustard greens or broccoli.

TOMATOES

Tomatoes are often sour and tasteless, so who can blame children for rejecting them? Buy sweet vine tomatoes - not expensive on market stalls - whenever you can. In any case, try sprinkling them with finely chopped fresh parsley to give a sweeter taste. If this doesn't work, then *very* secretly, sprinkle with a tiny pinch of caster sugar - a small compromise to make them acceptable. It often works!

Peeled tomatoes taste much nicer, so if your cook has the time, ask her to peel them and then chop or slice them.

Make a salad of skinned tomatoes with diced cucumber and avocado, tossed in a little olive oil and a *tiny* drop of lemon juice. Add a pinch of sugar and leave to marinate for a while.

Serve sliced tomatoes on toast: first grill one side of the bread, then turn the slices over, cover with cheese, grill for about half a minute, then cover the cheese with tomato slices and grill very slowly so the tomatoes partly caramelise. Perhaps sprinkle with finely chopped basil, parsley or chives.

Ratatouille: make it with fried onions, diced aubergines, a sliced courgette or two, a few red or yellow peppers and lots of ripe tomatoes. Add mixed herbs and a dash of ketchup. Serve with white fish, chicken and lamb. Wonderful at hiding the dry taste of liver. Serve with rice, pasta or potato.

Vegetable Minestrone: cook lots of sliced (or diced) carrots, celery, cabbage and onion in a mixture of tinned tomatoes and stock (you could use tinned consommé), with peas, sage and thyme. When done, stir in tinned haricot beans, and small pieces of cooked pasta – perhaps broken up spaghetti. Perhaps add shredded ham or crumbled minced beef. The soup should be thick with vegetables. Serve with plenty of grated cheese – Cheddar or Gouda are fine.

Tomato sauce: the most popular way of serving tomatoes is as tomato sauce. Make it thick and luscious. Stew plenty of chopped onion and a little garlic with a bay leaf in olive oil until soft. Tip in lots of tinned tomatoes along with all the juice, and mash down somewhat with a potato masher. Add good pinches of sage, thyme, parsley and basil (or mixed herbs), black pepper, and a minuscule pinch of cayenne. Bubble, stirring often, until the sauce is thick. Add some tomato purée and ketchup. If it tastes sour, add more ketchup or a pinch of sugar.

Serve this sauce generously on pizzas, or on toast, perhaps with grated cheese on top and grilled, or in pasta dishes, or with white fish, sardines, chicken, lamb, pork, or with haricot or kidney beans.

FRESH FRUIT

Serve it at snack time and for dessert. Arrange for staff to take one or two children shopping regularly for fruit. Some nurseries ask parents to donate fruit on an informal basis. A 'Fruit Basket' is put out for donations, and later the staff sort it, wash it and use it for the day's snacks.

Do serve fruit fully ripe! Bananas are not ripe until their skins are speckled with black. Pears and plums are usually rock hard when you buy them. Order fruit *at least* one week ahead, so it has time to ripen. Pears can take two or three weeks. Unripe fruit is harder for children to chew and digest and is less enjoyable.

<u>Fruit yoghurt:</u> wash the fruit, peel if necessary, then chop or purée it into plain, unsugared yoghurt. Add a little orange juice to sweeten, and *perhaps,* and only if essential, a little honey or sugar. Adding a few sultanas may provide sufficient extra sweetness. Add spices to cut tartness, for example mixed spice with blackberries or apricots, cinnamon and nutmeg with apples.

<u>Fruit platter:</u> cover a serving plate with small pieces of fruit such as: apple slices, orange segments or slices, banana chunks (peeled or not), grapefruit or satsuma segments, quartered, stoned plums, peaches and nectarines, quartered kiwis, thin

wedges or chunks of pineapple, melon or watermelon, whole strawberries, raspberries or blackberries... as fun finger food. See what's available in season and fully ripe and sweet. Let children help themselves (see pages 79-80). Sometimes put out just one or two fruits, sometimes more.

Sometimes serve whole fruits such as satsumas, blackberries, seedless grapes or small apples, as a change. Pile them into a pyramid or another shape.

Serve slices of apple, or of ripe, juicy pears with thin curls of Parmesan or Cheddar cheese as a meal ending.

Cook mixtures of fruits, sometimes with a little spice (for example, cook dessert apples with raspberries or with blackberries with mixed spice, or cook apricots with raisins and cinnamon), and add a very little sugar. Serve as it is, warm or cold. Offer yoghurt, evaporated milk or custard to stir into the fruit mixture, or serve with rice pudding. Or make a fruit crumble, or a pie with just a top crust, and serve with custard or evaporated milk.

Make a thick layer of fruit on top of a cheesecake.

Make banana custard with lots of banana slices. Vary the fruit: make strawberry or raspberry custard (scrumptious cold in summer!), or apricot, raisin and cinnamon custard, warm or cold.

Serve kiwi fruit halves in egg cups to eat with a teaspoon.

'Fruit smoothie': in a liquidiser, blend lots of sweet fruit such as banana with plain yoghurt, fresh orange juice, a drop of honey, vanilla, nutmeg and milk.

Fruit jelly: pack layers of fruit into a deep container, and pour over a jelly mixture made with orange juice and gelatine (or agar-agar). Let set, then unmould for a spectacular-looking pudding. Serve with yoghurt.

Mango fool: purée fresh mango (or tinned, draining off the syrup), and mix with custard and orange juice. Marble in some plain yoghurt.

Marinate chopped strawberries in fresh orange juice. Serve with yoghurt or custard.

Make ice-cream with cooked, puréed fruit, orange juice and yoghurt or evaporated milk.

Have fruit lollipops as a treat: freeze hunks of banana or satsuma/orange segments.

If a good selection of fruit is unavailable or too expensive, use frozen or tinned. For example, whisk thawed mixed summer fruits into custard or yoghurt for a good pudding, hot or cold. Or serve bread and butter with soft summer fruits or stewed fruit.

EXAMPLES OF MENUS

It is assumed that children in half-day care will be given one main meal (lunch) and either a mid-morning or mid-afternoon snack. Children in full-day care (8 hours or more) should be offered a more substantial meal in the afternoon, here referred to as 'tea'.

These menus assume that children are drinking at least 200ml (one third of a pint) of full fat milk at nursery, in addition to that built into menus. Children who don't drink milk for whatever reason need plenty of food involving milk and milk products, and/or other calcium-rich foods (see page 33).

Detailed weekly menus should be displayed in advance for parents, with any changes put in so parents always know what has been served. Parents should be told what food has been eaten each day, and how well their child has eaten.

BREAKFAST

Breakfast is a very important meal. It is recommended that parents and guardians and those providing child care should work together to make sure that children have breakfast.

Some ideas:

- *toast with cheese, egg, tomatoes, or (reduced sugar & salt) baked beans*

- *breakfast cereals which do not have added sugar. Try wholewheat ones such as puffed wheat, Weetabix or Shredded Wheat. For a change, try low-sugar 'fortified' cereals, such as cornflakes, crisped rice or wheatbiscs (at least 15g). Serve cereals with whole milk (warm or cold). Never add sugar at the table. Try Weetabix spread with butter or a good sunflower margarine – very crumbly to eat but fun!*

- *porridge made with all milk and with a dab of honey, but with plenty of chopped banana and/or sultanas. It will taste sweet but not rot teeth. Before serving, add full fat evaporated (not sweetened condensed) milk to turn it into a luscious, creamy-tasting treat*

- *wheat germ porridge: wheat germ (e.g. Bemax) stirred into warm milk*

- *pieces of fruit, either fresh or tinned in juice, perhaps with evaporated milk, as an extra*

- *to drink: milk (at least 100ml), warm if the children like it, and diluted real orange juice (at least 25ml before diluting)*

- *variety! Have something different each day of the week.*

Occasionally put in something new such as fruit muffins, warm crumpets or bacon

---

DINNER MENUS

Ideas for main courses for one month:

Also have a vegetarian option if the main dish contains meat or fish. If possible, have extra salads and vegetables on offer as a choice.

Mon: *Curried vegetable stir-fry; dhal; rice; popadums, chapattis or nan*

Tue: *Jamaican chicken (mixed vegetables, wholewheat pasta, beansprouts)†*

Wed: *Pizza with tomato sauce, mushrooms, sardines & mozzarella*†; green salad*

Thurs: *Grilled mackerel with apricot sauce*; mashed potatoes*

Fri: *Broccoli and cauliflower cheese*; sautéed potatoes; roast tomato slices*

Mon: *Rainbow stir-fry (red & yellow peppers, carrot, broccoli, onion, celery, with mozzarella cheese), wholewheat pasta or couscous*

Tues: *Steak & kidney pie with mushrooms; mashed potato, carrot 'red mountain'*, green vegetables in season*

Wed: *Hungarian fish casserole†; mashed sweet potato or rice; green beans*

Thurs: *Chicken casserole with onions, carrots & celery; carrot & swede purée; bubble and squeak*

Fri: *Soup & quiche day: home-made minestrone*† with grated Gouda; home-made quiche with bacon and cheese*†, jacket potatoes, lettuce leaf salad*

Mon: *Golden sesame slices†; Brussels sprout 'green mountain'; mashed potato*

Tue: *Lasagne (beef or soya mince, tomato sauce*†, cheese sauce†, spinach, mushrooms); green salad*

Wed: *Caribbean red bean stew (peppers, tomato, onion, cabbage)†; rice*

Thurs: *Filo pastry pie, layered with assorted vegetables and cheese; mashed potato*

Fri: *Fish cakes†; tomato sauce*†; peas; oven chips*

Mon: *Spaghetti sauce with chicken livers, mushrooms and tomato purée*†; wholewheat spaghetti; crunchy green salad*

Tue: *Bean and cauliflower bake†; mashed potatoes*

Wed: *Sweet and sour Chinese vegetable stir-fry; fried tofu; noodles*

Thurs: *Whiting in home-made cheese sauce; mushrooms, mashed potato; peas*

Fri: *Finger food day: marinated chicken drumsticks; hot garlic bread; stir-fried carrot and celeriac sticks; broccoli florets*

---

* a recipe outline may be found under the general heading 'The best use of the best foods' beginning on page 52.

† the recipe may be found in *The Nursery Food Book* (see page 132).

For desserts: Please see pages 62-64 for ideas for serving fruit.

SNACKS

Energetic children may well run out of energy between one meal and the next. Arrange for a snack time mid way between meals to give time for appetites to work up to the next meal. Allow for no more than 2-2$^{1}/_{2}$ hours without offering a meal or snack.

- *always offer at least 100ml (3 fl oz) of milk*

- *always have water on offer*

- *offer fresh fruit and/or vegetable sticks*

- *have something more substantial too such as chunks of bread which children can break up with their fingers, or breadsticks, oatcakes or scones, perhaps with a plate of thin slices of cheese*

TEA TIME

These ideas are for nurseries who serve tea as a meal (that is, not just a snack) in the late afternoon. (But see page 85.)

- *Make bread the basis of nursery tea. Put out a variety of breads, preferably as chunks, as in snacks, above. Hot toast with a good topping makes a good winter tea.*

- *Always serve milk, but also offer water, diluted fruit juice, and, occasionally, other drinks such as hot chocolate, or a milk or fruit shake (see pages 57 and 63).*

- *Offer a choice of food. One day's selection could be: cheese sticks, curd cheese, pieces of chicken, hard boiled egg, celeriac sticks, radishes, hummus, and slices of melon and orange.*

- *Always have a choice of fresh fruit.*

Ideas for tea time dishes:

- *hot toast with either scrambled or boiled eggs; home-made tomato sauce (see page 61); cheese slices; grilled cheese perhaps with tomato slices; sardines, pilchards, tinned cod's roe, fish paste (see page 55) or liver paté with lettuce; tuna with sweetcorn; honey and tahini; low salt and sugar baked beans*

- *sandwiches, open or closed, with fillings such as chopped egg with mayonnaise and cress; tuna and sweetcorn; curd cheese and diced celery or ham; curd cheese with raspberries, apricots, banana, grapes or other soft fruits; herb cheese with cucumber; cold chicken; cheese sticks and lettuce; mashed banana; slices of omelette and lettuce; sliced tomato, avocado & curd cheese; any salad items such as radishes, tomato, peppers, beetroot, cress, carrot sticks. Children could help themselves from a choice of fillings:*

- *warmed pitta pockets with a choice of fillings, such as above*

- *jacket potato with a choice of fillings such as above*

- *Portuguese salad (see page 54)*

- *home-made carrot cake, banana bread, cheesecake or fruit biscuits*

- *toasted tea-cake, fruit buns or scones, with cheese slices*

- *fruit bread, buttered, or with cheese slices*

- *onion bhajis, samosas, spring rolls, felafel (occasionally – these are fatty foods)*

- *warmed cheese scones, pizza slices, quiche slices*

- *baby meatballs or fish rissoles*

- *muffins, oatcakes, crumpets*

GUIDE TO PORTION SIZES FOR THREE YEAR OLDS

Although some children need to eat more than others, below are some examples of portion sizes for an 'average' three year old at a main meal. Older children may need considerably more. Aim for a small surplus of food to be sure there is plenty.

Shepherd's pie	*150g*	*Potatoes*	*60g*
Tuna, beans and sweetcorn pasta		*Stir-fried vegetables*	*80g*
	140g	*Broccoli*	*40g*
Chicken and vegetable curry	*100g*	*Carrots*	*40g*
Slice of quiche	*100g*	*Peas*	*30g*
Lamb burger	*80g*	*Milk*	*100ml*
potato curry	*60g*	*Orange juice (before diluting)*	*25ml*
Rice	*80g*	*Fruit*	*80g*
Dhal	*50g*	*Dried fruit salad*	*100g*
Chapatti	*20g*	*Cooked fruit pudding*	*60-80g*
Pasta	*80g*	*Rice pudding*	*100g*

Compiled from the menu suggestions in 'Eating Well for Under-Fives in Child Care' by kind permission of the Caroline Walker Trust.

It is a good idea to have a written food policy. Most nurseries already have some kind of unwritten policy, but in writing it down, everyone has a chance to agree to the ideas. The policy should be displayed and also included in your new parents' Welcome Pack. Most policies will need to change over time with experience and as new issues arise and staff change, so the policy should be reviewed periodically and rewritten as necessary.

The sample policy below is a guide to the sort of information a nursery may wish to include, suggested by The Caroline Walker Trust, and reproduced by kind permission from their 'Eating Well for Under-Fives in Child Care'.

SAMPLE NUTRITION POLICY

- *The weekly menu will be available in advance. Recipes will be available to parents*

- *The weekly menu will provide children with a tasty and varied diet*

- *All the children in child care will have suitable food made available for them*

- *Children who do not receive breakfast at home will be offered this when they arrive if this has been agreed with their parents or guardians*

- *Milk will be served at morning and afternoon snacks*

- *All dairy products will be full-fat*

- *Soya milks will only be given as a substitute for cows' milk with the parents' agreement, and then only those fortified with calcium*

- *Water will be available at all times*

- *Diluted fruit juice will be served with the main meal*

- *Children will have access to bread and fruit if they are hungry between meals*

- *Children will be allowed to have second helpings of fruit and milk-based desserts*

- *Children will still be given dessert even if they refuse their main course*

- *Parents or guardians will be advised if their child is not eating well*

- *Parents of children who are on special diets will be asked to provide as much information as possible about suitable foods, and in some cases may be asked to provide the food themselves*

- *Carers will sit with children while they eat and will provide a good role model for healthy eating*

- *Withholding food will not be used as a form of punishment*

- *Children will be encouraged to develop good eating skills and table manners and be given plenty of time to eat*

- *Advice will be given to parents about suitable food to bring from home*

- *Children will be encouraged to play outside each day, weather permitting. This will ensure they have an opportunity to be exposed to summer sunlight which helps their bodies to make vitamin D*

4: WHO WILL COOK THE FOOD?

THE LYNCH PIN in providing good food is the cook. Do your utmost to get your nursery the best cook or caterers possible, so many food problems won't even arise. What are the possibilities?

THE NURSERY'S OWN COOK

Having your own cook is by far the best idea. However, you need someone who understands a nursery's particular needs. Some cooks who are used to cooking in larger institutions may have little idea about cooking for 30 under fives. In this situation, the food should be home cooking rather than mass catering, but this might seem strange to someone conventionally experienced. She may want to stock up with frozen chips and ready-made mixes and fillings, all quite unsuitable for a nursery.

Finding a really good cook may be difficult, but it's worth trying to locate someone who would enjoy such a job - perhaps a retired restaurant cook looking for something to do, or someone between jobs, or a newly qualified chef without a job. Even someone not planning to stay long may like the job and decide to stay longer. Meanwhile, your meals could be terrific. Advertise in your nearest catering college and talk to the head of department. Ask colleagues in other nurseries and care centres. A parent may have a suggestion. Let people know you are looking. It's fair to both sides to employ a new cook on a month's mutual 'probation'.

It is up to the manager to explain the nursery's food ethos, and answer any questions the cook may have about it. Do:

- explain that small children need 'home cooking', not institutional fare: shortcrust pastry and scones, for example, should be made entirely from fresh ingredients and not from mixes. Ready-made fillings and mixes are similarly unnecessary, and probably too additive-laden, salty and spiced up for young children anyway. Although adults may enjoy well-seasoned food, children generally like something simpler. Real food cooked from scratch from basic ingredients is the idea.

- say the food should comply with current healthy eating guidelines, and explain exactly what that means for your nursery. Perhaps give her a copy of this book: the ideas in chapter three might be helpful. For recipes, you could give her a copy of **The Nursery Food Book** (see page 132). Explain why such foods as chips, burgers, 'nuggets', sausages, crisps, bottled drinks, jelly, biscuits and ready-made mixes are not appropriate.

- be tactful. It is not her personal fault that atrocious food is so prevalent in institutions. In the event, she may be delighted to do more real cooking, and to be able to use and develop her skills for such a worthwhile purpose. Point out this advantage.

- you could add that this type of food **and** the way of serving it (see page 79) will probably mean less work. For example, serving fresh fruit for dessert is easier than cooking a pudding every day, and deep frying may be a job she will be glad to dispense with.

- your aim is to find someone who can cook well, who will have a loyalty towards you and who will stay. Make her feel an intrinsic part of the nursery staff and stress the huge contribution to children's well being that a good cook can make. Discuss the menus, recipes and the food order together. Include her in staff meetings when you discuss food, recognising that her hours may be different from those of other staff.

- if she has to adapt her cooking style and learn new recipes, be reasonable about allowing her a little time to change. In any case, if the nursery needs to change to a better way of eating, it's wise to make the changes slowly and all move forward together.

- acknowledge her existing skills and praise her for what she does well. When the nursery's food is praised, tell her about it. Make sure she is given fair credit. If she's good, it's in your *interests she feels appreciated and wants to stay. Would she enjoy going on any local courses to improve her skills?*

LOCAL AUTHORITY CATERERS

The situation with local authority caterers varies from place to place, and the quality of food may depend on whether your local authority caterers are in house or not. In-house caterers tend to be better and it could be easier to influence them.

However, every authority should have its official healthy eating guidelines which should fit in with government ones. Get hold of a copy of your authority's guidelines, but don't be surprised if they are vague.

Since April 2000, tendering for catering contracts now comes under 'Best Value', the successor to Compulsory Competitive Tendering (CCT), and local authorities will have the obligation to consult before tendering. The thing is not to miss any consultation opportunity. At present, few nurseries seem to respond when their local authority routinely asks them for their opinions! Make your voice heard. Write in early. Take as active a part as possible in the consultation process.

If you can't wait until you are formally asked, write now. The person to contact is the Client Officer, who is usually employed by either the education or social services department. Telephone and ask for a meeting to discuss things. It may be useful to invite the officer to visit you. If, for example, your food is difficult for younger children to manage, a lunch time visit could demonstrate this. Aim for a good personal relationship, which can only be beneficial. Also, try to talk directly to the cook.

The situation may be more difficult if your authority employs outside caterers. Your authority may say they must accept the 'most economical' (i.e. lowest) tender. This doesn't of itself mean that the food has to be poor, though it may be. Inspections may be both rare and useless. Whatever can you do?

• *Don't feel at the caterer's mercy! Use consumer power - you are a customer after all. Don't believe that they cannot buy this or that: they have access to exactly the same range of wholesale produce as shopkeepers do, and furthermore they buy in bulk, with discount. Of course they can provide nectarines and raspberries in summer! Buying seasonally is cheap, and there are always bargains to be had. The idea that varied, healthy food is impossibly expensive should be countered vigorously and with evidence.*

Caterers find it simpler, of course, to put the same food order in month in month out ignoring both seasonality and variety. To many caterers, 'fresh fruit' means only oranges, Golden Delicious apples and (usually) unripe bananas, these hard fruits being the easiest for them to handle. Some caterers say that ending a meal with fresh fruit is 'too expensive'. This is nonsense of course - it's simply less effort for them to sell ready-made, low-nutrient 'desserts'. But caterers are being paid for a service - sometimes very well - and should be called to account when they fail you.

• *If you are unhappy with any aspect of the food, tell the caterers directly. Be courteous, but make your point clearly and don't be fobbed off. By all means sympathise with their problems, but point out that their meals do not fit in with local authority guidelines, or that the children won't eat this or that, and state which changes you want. Be precise and suggest reasonable alternatives - and try to agree a date for the change. Disregard old chestnuts like 'everyone else likes it' and 'no one has complained before'.*

• *If this doesn't work, contact your local Client Officer. Telephone or write, and try to talk to him or her in person.*

• *You could also talk to your local authority's community dietitians or nutritionists at the Dietetics Department of your district hospital. Show them your menus, describe the size of portions and so on, and get them to help you put in a complaint.*

• *If your problem is sugary desserts and snacks, or drinks containing sugar or citric acid, you could contact their Dental Department.*

• *Meanwhile, you don't have to serve everything the caterer sends. If something is really appalling, send it back, with an appropriate letter, rather than serving it.*

• *If you are having a new caterer, influence their contract via the Client Officer, and get the specification as tight as possible. Be determined! Consider sharing a caterer with other local nurseries or schools and negotiate together.*

• *If you do have good caterers, give them praise - and further suggestions. Keep up a good relationship and things could get even better!*

PRIVATE CATERERS

With private caterers you have more control, although the problem of finding someone good remains. Catering for less than 200 means low profits for most caterers, so you may have difficulties. Use the general advice as above while you search for somebody local who could prepare meals for you. Find out what the going rate is, ask around, advertise - and be prepared to pay a little more.

• *Negotiate a contract with them. Give them a copy of the current healthy-eating guidelines in case they don't have one - or have never been asked to consider this aspect before.*

• *Ask for a month's **summertime** menus. And ask 'How often do you turn the menus around?' Menus should not be turned around (repeated) in less time than one month, and there is no reason for not having seasonal food. If the fruit turns out to be just apples, oranges and bananas, you'll know they're not thinking seasonally. If the type of fruit is not stipulated, ask.*

• *It may be better if two or three nurseries (or other care centres) negotiate a contract together.*

• *Be very clear about what you want. Specify fresh fruit for dessert every day, and a certain minimum of fresh vegetables over the week. Say 'Chips only once a month', 'No burgers' and so on.*

• *Specify that there must be choices within each day's menu.*

• *Specify that there must be **enough** food - including proper* *adult portions for staff.*

• *Teatime meals should be meals not snacks.*

• *Specify that multicultural needs and special diets, including vegetarian choices, will be properly catered for.*

• *Discuss the time schedule. Staff need to be able to rely on the food being on time and children need to eat without being rushed.*

• *Sort out any details that are not completely clear. After the contract is signed it could be difficult to make further changes.*

• *Be realistic. Ask as many caterers as possible, and ask around for opinions and recommendations. Don't find you've just rejected the best of the bunch just because you didn't realize they were the best!*

Whoever caters for you, keep them up to standard. Assess the food critically. Read food labels regularly and check ingredients for sugar, salt and fat levels and number of additives. Check use-by dates. Never, never, 'leave it to the cook'. Children's priorities come before caterers' convenience.

5: ORGANISING HAPPY MEALTIMES

THE CHILD-CENTRED, informal atmosphere that should exist throughout the day should also continue at mealtimes. Although dinner time (especially) necessarily involves adult timetables and other constraints, such pressures should not be apparent to the children. Of course dinner time has its own special routine, but from a child's point of view, it should appear as just another enjoyable event in their day.

Perhaps unsurprisingly, children have been found to thrive noticeably better when they regularly eat in a happy atmosphere. If mealtimes are to be enjoyable, there are various aspects to consider apart from the actual quality and taste of the food.

MAKE THE DINING AREA LOOK INVITING

Turning the dining tables at 45° to the walls looks informal and attractive. Do have tablecloths (pretty plastic, or cotton ones covered with a sheet of translucent plastic) and possibly place mats as well. Have flowers on the tables in little pots, or, in winter, seasonal greenery, dried flowers, or bulbs growing in pots or glass hyacinth 'sprouters'. Think of your colour scheme – do the tablecloths, plates, pinafores and napkins fit in with the decor of the room? Will they complement the food? Of course the area should look clean and reasonably tidy, setting the scene for a pleasant mealtime ahead.

An interesting feature incorporated into one or two newly-built nurseries is to have the kitchen alongside the dining area. The children can thus see all the cooking and clearing up being done before, during and after mealtimes. When children do cooking activities, such nearby access to ovens could be a boon, even though children should not go into the kitchen itself for safety reasons.

The appearance of the food itself is crucial. When the food is put on each table, it should look immediately attractive. Try to see it through children's eyes. Who can blame children for refusing greens that have turned limp and grey?

Enliven dishes by adding a few parsley sprigs, pastry 'leaves' or tassels, a dusting of paprika, edible flowers or petals (e.g. English marigold, pansy, rose, or any herb flowers), a criss-cross pattern of chive blades or a border of cucumber, orange, lemon or kiwi slices. Always put either carrot or red pepper (or both) into your stir-fries for their colour, and anything with a golden brown topping looks enticing. Arrange slices of apple or orange and satsuma segments into swirl patterns on the plate. Perhaps the cook can think of some whimsical touches such as making faces with pieces of tomato on jacket potatoes, or making fish 'swim' on waves of shredded lettuce. All garnishes must be edible in case they get eaten.

Notice if children are put off by the way food is presented. For example, children like to see what they're getting and can be put off if foods are too mixed up: they may not like fish pie, but enjoy fish and potato served separately. The food should not be too hot or the children could burn their tongues. Younger children may not realise how hot something is, and hungry children may not have the patience to wait anyway.

KEEP IT CALM

It is lovely if lunch time can be a period of relative calm in the middle of a busy day. Staff should talk quietly and encourage children to do the same. If adults call out to one another why should children not do so? Listen critically to all the sounds in the room at lunch time and see which ones would be better reduced, such as kitchen clatter. Could a noisy fan be switched off while the children are eating? (The radio certainly must be!) Lining metal trays with a thin layer of plastic foam or bubble wrap hugely lessens the din if cutlery is tossed in.

The children will be more ready to settle down if they have been active beforehand and also if they have had good notice that it will soon be time to eat, so their play is not abruptly stopped. A brief, quiet time immediately before eating, perhaps on the mat, can help.

HOW WILL YOU SERVE THE FOOD?

There are two ways: either have the food put out in serving bowls on each table for children to help themselves, or have a 'buffet table' for children to help themselves. Generally, lunches and any tea time meals (i.e. not just snacks) are best with food put on the table, but at other times children can choose their food from a buffet and take it to eat at a table or on a seat or mat, depending on your situation. In summer, aim to eat some food outside.

LUNCH TIME

Have about six children sitting around a table along with a member of staff. The table should be ready laid with cutlery, possibly napkins, and serving implements. There also need to be beakers, and a water jug on the table or nearby. (Children can

help lay tables, perhaps on a rota.) Family meals are unknown to some children, so it can be a new and very educational experience for such children to have a round-the-table meal with others. For children who may be fed on their own at home, perhaps being left in front of the television while the adults go to do something else, sociable nursery meals are especially important.

The adult may have to cut up certain foods (whilst sitting with the children, not standing and leaning over them), after which the children simply help themselves. They should be encouraged to do this as soon as they are physically able – from about the age of two. There are four rules:

Fair shares
Fair shares is the first essential rule. Obviously, no one has to eat all of their fair share of what's available, but no one can have *more* than that unless there's a genuine surplus. Having understood that, children help themselves to as much or as little as they wish of whatever is on the table.

Good food
If it's all good, nutritious food, there should be no worry about someone having too much of anything. If a child eats lots of one particular food for a while, she will probably tire of it later on and go for something else. Children may like to eat foods they don't often (or ever) get at home, or that they have a nutritional need for at that time. Allow them to choose; you can't always know what's behind a preference.

No criticisms!
Staff should not criticise children's choices or amounts of food chosen. Children's appetites vary with spurts of growth – and for various other reasons including feeling unhappy or being off-colour. Also, they may try to play staff up or get extra attention over refusing food, especially if they have got into this habit at home. But it is counterproductive and often distressing for a child to be urged to eat something he doesn't want. Staff should notice if someone is eating very little, or choosing a very restricted diet over a period of time, but not *seem* to be paying any attention to it. Usually, when children realise that no comments are going to be made one way or the other, they relax and eat better. Any criticisms from other children should be stopped (see also page 83).

Sociability
Mealtimes should be pleasant, relaxed and unhurried, with time

for children to chat with each other and with staff. It can be a useful and pleasant way for staff to get to know individual children.

You may inherit a nursery where staff dish the food up onto children's plates. If so, changing to the help-yourself way could be a priority. It has various advantages, including making less work for staff and increasing children's involvement in the meal, which can result in their eating better. It is obviously better if children can see a whole dish before it's cut up, instead of seeing it only as a lump of something or other on their plates, which in turn gives the cook an incentive to present the food in an attractive way, which is otherwise pointless. The appearance of a dish can in itself stimulate appetite.

A LEARNING SITUATION

At mealtimes, children learn about the sociable aspects of eating, and staff should help them to acquire basic table manners such as asking politely for something and using cutlery correctly. In this respect, staff should set a good example. Mealtimes also help children to learn about numbers, colours, halves and quarters, 'right and left', the names of various foods and dishes and how to lay a table. Seeing a dish divided into portions provides an excellent introduction to fractions, volume and capacity. Children can quickly learn to work out their fair share!

Opportunities exist for learning about healthy eating. Research has shown that young children are often interested in learning about food and its relation to nutrition and health. A few hygiene rules can also be learned, such as taking a second helping with the serving spoon and not with the spoon they have been eating with, and not coughing or sneezing over food.

Staff should not talk about slimming in front of children. These days, even young children can think of any kind of chubbiness as 'fat', and try to limit their food.

NO PRESSURE

Some children will be tasting foods they have never eaten, or even seen, before. Remember that everyone needs time to get used to a new taste. A child who rejects sweet potatoes because they are completely strange, may, if *unpressured*, eventually help herself to a spoonful, and later may decide she likes it and take more. This might take a few minutes or several encounters with the food. Seeing other people – including staff – eating it with enjoyment, without feeling she is in the wrong for not doing so, is the best encouragement. Staff could very gently suggest she might like to taste a tiny bit, adding 'If you don't like it just leave it, it doesn't matter', but this must be done very lightly and with sensitive regard to the child in question. If she decides she just doesn't like it, that choice should be respected. (Think which foods *you* dislike, and how you would feel if someone were repeatedly urging you to try them again. We let ourselves off lightly over our likes and dislikes, but can be quite determined with children.)

It never works to bribe, cajole, threaten, punish or in any way try to force children to eat something they don't want, and it is unprofessional. The usual outcome is that children will hate it even more and may also very quickly hate the adults who put them through such misery. A child may even begin to fear coming to nursery because of worry about mealtime pressures. Conversely, when children feel free to choose what and how much they eat, they become more adventurous and also tend to eat more.

It is easy to feel angry, even personally affronted, when a child refuses food. Staff may worry that children who seem to eat very little may become unhealthy or underweight, although such fears are usually groundless. They may also worry about 'wasted food', or the 'waste of the parents' money'. Staff must understand how quickly children can become distressed by attempts to make them 'eat up'. We should not try to make children eat until *we* feel satisfied.

By the age of four, most children are capable of helping themselves to the amount they can eat, after a little practice. Of course, some children will need more food than others. For example, children who are destined to be tall have a lot of growing to do and have extra 'building blocks' to make. Be careful of labelling such children either 'greedy', or making their 'good' appetites a matter for special praise. Like smaller eaters, they are simply – and correctly – eating what their bodies are telling them they need. Labelling a child a 'good eater' could cause the child to overeat in an effort to retain enjoyable praise. Children should be encouraged to eat until they've had enough, *whatever that is,* and to learn to stop at that point. Thus, the amount of food left on a child's plate (if any) becomes of no consequence.

Staff should not allow children to criticise each others' choices. For example, if a child says 'She's only got a tiny bit!', the swift (and pleasantly spoken) response could be 'Yes, she took what she wanted, just like you took what you wanted', followed by a change of subject. New children may take a while before they feel like eating much. The sooner they realise there's no pressure, the sooner they'll feel comfortable about eating. Meanwhile, offer them food, be prepared to take no for an answer and chat as usual with other children on the table, including the new child in the conversation. Treat attention-seekers and 'fussy' eaters the same way. Ignore their fuss as much as possible, keep the meal pleasant, and chat about other things.

Of course conversation about how delicious something tastes is another matter. Staff could say 'You *did* enjoy that, didn't you', to a child who is scraping her plate, or say 'I can see you like broccoli as much as I do' (N.B. broccoli non-fans must *pretend*!). Such remarks have often been found to encourage nearby reluctant eaters to eat more. Keep such remarks positive but not pointed. If a reluctant or fussy eater does eventually try something different, praise him gently, no matter how little he ate.

One extra point is worth mentioning concerning the texture of food. Child psychologist Dr. Richard Woolfson says 'Remember that children vomit more easily than adults. Food which is too dry or sticky can stick to their upper palate, making them sick. Children can't help this reaction. Avoid textures that the child has already said she dislikes or you are heading for trouble.'

If an item of food is actually unpleasant and no one is enjoying it, just say something like 'What a shame. I'll just eat a *little* bit of it. It's usually nice, isn't it. I cook it at home sometimes'. There is no point in insisting something is nice when it patently is not. On the other hand, personal dislikes by staff (there could be several!) should be well hidden in case children pick them up and decide they don't like fish purely because their favourite staff member doesn't. If the adults are seen to eat everything, they may well be copied. Remember, children love to imitate. It is useful for staff to listen to children's comments about the food. It can be instructive and can reveal areas for improvement.

In all, keep mealtimes pleasant, strictly fair, and keep out any fuss – from children or from staff.

TEA-TIME AND SNACKS

'Tea-time' in this section refers to a sizeable meal for children in an all-day setting. Nurseries running a shorter day need not serve a meal to children shortly before they go home. This gives mothers the opportunity to prepare food themselves for their children and not feel they have lost a role now the children are at nursery, as can happen. However, children should not be sent home ravenous as this could lead to sugary snacks being given on the way home. The nursery could offer a light snack 1-2 hours before the children leave. Any snacks the nursery serves may be presented as follows:

Put the food on a low table so children can reach it easily. There may or may not be a need for plates, depending on what is served. Small knives are useful if the children are going to make their own sandwiches. Arrange for as much choice as possible. For example, instead of having sandwiches ready made, put out a choice of bread and the various fillings so children can make their own, open or closed. This is excellent for improving fine motor skills, and most children will soon become adept. The free choice and variety of foods, as well as seeing others trying different things, encourage children to try new foods.

One day's menu could consist, for example, of cheese sticks, pieces of chicken, curd cheese, pineapple pieces, satsuma segments, watercress sprigs, radishes and apple slices with a choice of buns, bread and crackers. Any combination the children wish to try is good; it's not for staff to say 'You don't eat satsumas with cheese!' or whatever. Sometimes children like to experiment with food tastes as with other things. There could be a home-made milk shake (see pages 57 and 63) as well as diluted fruit juice, milk and plain water. In colder weather, offer hot wholewheat toast (perhaps with beans, scrambled egg or cheese on top), vegetable soup, slices of pizza, toasted fruit buns or scones and maybe hot chocolate. Keep tea-time food different from lunch in style and format as well as foodstuffs.

Children can take their chosen food and drink to a table or to some other designated area such as a mat, or outside, depending on your situation. Eat-and-come-again, as with any buffet. Some children may eat something, go back to their play activity and then come back for more. Such informality is pleasant and fits in with the child's own pace.

As with lunch tables, children can help to lay the buffet table and help clear away. It's good social training as well as practice with the concept of one-to-one correspondence. The nursery could designate two helpers, with their names posted up, each day.

Avoid queues and a crush, so especially if the nursery is large, have the buffet 'open' over a period of time. It's better to allow children to come for food when they're hungry – including allowing them not to come, or to come for very little – than to try and herd them in all at once. You could also stagger the time for different groups of children, or have the food on more than one table in different places so the children spread out. Try not to let the convenience of the kitchen and your timetable take undue precedence over the children. If a child is very engrossed at snack time, a glass of milkshake or a sandwich could be put where the child is working to avoid interrupting their activity too much. Children are not at nursery to be institutionalised. Always look to see how things can be made more home-like.

As for hand washing beforehand, try to avoid queues and institutionalised mass-handwashing. Perhaps wash-cloths could be available in the playroom near the food for all but the dirtiest hands.

KEEP IT ACTIVE

The usual mealtime pattern is for children to be firmly sat down while the adults do all the work, possibly getting flustered and possibly getting cross. It is also boring and pointless for children to be left sitting or standing about with nothing to do while they wait for the adults to serve them, and mischief, disputes and tears can easily result.

Timing is crucial, but it can feel better all round if children do at least some of the jobs, and letting children help themselves at table saves work for staff. Making children feel they are partly responsible for their own food leads to a better atmosphere and children will often eat a previously disliked food when they have cooked it themselves. Organise a plan of who helps to do what.

THE IMPORTANCE OF EXERCISE

Children should be hungry for their meal.

It may seem obvious to say that children should look forward to mealtimes and be eager to eat, but it depends to a considerable extent on how active they are. A study in the Bristol-Avon area shows that even though they are eating less, pre-school children are getting fatter. Indeed, the report found an alarming proportion of under-fives are overweight, and obese, because, it seems, they are taking less exercise. Exercise is needed for good muscle development and to work up an appetite. The more exercise children get the more they will need to eat and the more nutrients they can obtain. Sedentary children with small appetites may be going short of nutrients.

Parental fears of letting children go outside to play, driving them to school and to other venues, and the presence of television and computer games can all contribute to too little exercise and reduced appetite. At nursery, where children are well supervised in an enclosed area, staff should ensure that full use is made of the outdoor space, and encourage children to be active, to run about, to feel warm, to get out of breath – and to get hungry. As we all know, food tastes better when we're hungry! And hungry children are less picky and may eat more.

The nursery needs safe, well-maintained outdoor equipment such as hoops and large balls, as well as a climbing frame and other large scale equipment that involve pushing and pulling. Staff will need to check that climbing apparatus is not wet and slippery before children go on it. The Health Education Authority recommends that under-fives have half an hour to an hour every day of at least moderately intense physical activity. More is fine if children are enjoying themselves and if they can have food and a drink when they are hungry or thirsty. Short walks to a nearby park or playground where the children can enjoy slightly different activities are a good idea. Exercise needs to be built into the nursery's plan for each day throughout the year. Of course all activities must be well-supervised, and someone must be on duty outdoors when any children are outside.

Parents may need reminding about sending children in clothing that is suitable for playing outdoors at different times of year, including sending cotton sun hats and 'cover up' clothing for hot weather. Staff must then see that children are actually wearing their sun hats and that no one is getting hot because of wearing unnecessary layers, and, in winter, that children's hats, boots and mittens are worn and that their coats are properly buttoned up. Parents could be asked to send children in 'something thick and something thin', such as a T-shirt *and* a jumper, so their children can be comfortable according to changing temperatures and different levels of activity. Staff should also check for the safety of children's clothing, such as seeing that shoe laces are firmly tied and that scarves are tucked well inside coats so they cannot catch on something.

Nurseries with covered verandas for outdoor play in bad weather are fortunate, but every nursery should aim for some energetic activity and some fresh air each day. In impossible weather, arrange for lively indoor activities.

FLEXIBLE FUN

Build some variety into your mealtime routine. For example, in summer, when strawberries are at their best (and cheapest) have a Strawberry Day and serve a mound of them (with alternative fruit for anyone with a strawberry allergy or who might not want many). Make the most of the day, with

strawberry-based activities, such as making
paintings and papier maché models,
having a story and singing a song
about them (see page 112).

Try having an Italian Food
Day, a Chinese Day, a Caribbean
Day or a Scottish Day. Celebrate
Divali with special food. Try a
Pitta Pocket Day with warmed
brown and white pitta bread and a choice of fillings, or, in hot
weather, a 'Cold Cut' Day in which children help themselves to
pieces of chicken, ham, hard-boiled egg, haslet and sardines,
with a variety of salads and breads. Ask staff and parents for
ideas and recipes for a particular cuisine. If a new recipe is
popular it can go into the repertoire. Perhaps change the
arrangements of tables in the room for a special day. Have a
Picnic Day when meals are taken out of doors.

Having a visitor can be fun. If a parent has been helping in the
nursery that morning, she could perhaps be asked to stay for
dinner – something she may appreciate, especially when your
food is good! Of course you need to be confident about your
food, as well as your routine before, as it were, opening your
restaurant to inspection. In any case, discuss it with all your
staff beforehand, *and* ask the child concerned if he would like
his mother to stay – perhaps he wouldn't!

MAKING CHANGES

You may inherit a situation that needs improving. How best to
go about it? First be quite clear where exactly the faults lie,
decide *why* the situation is as it is (attitudes of staff, perhaps?),
and think what can be changed. Perhaps everything can be
changed – given sufficient time.

Having thought about it, discuss it with your staff. Say, for
example, that you are concerned about certain aspects of the
food or serving arrangement, and suggest some changes. You

may get ready agreement from some staff, but others may have little or even completely erroneous ideas of healthy eating and think things are fine as they are.

State your case and back it up – *The Nursery Food Book*, written for students and child carers, could be a useful book to have around. It states the case for healthy eating simply and has a fund of practical ideas. Make the book available for staff to read so they can see that it's not just your personal ideas that are in question – a book that is used in colleges says the same thing! Having a talk by your local authority's community dietitian might also be useful, and there may be local courses on the subject that staff might profit from.

It may be that older members of staff are more resistant to change and they, as well as the children, will need time to get used to a new régime. Usually, when they see that it is working, that the children and parents are happy with it – and that their own job is in some ways easier – resistance disappears. Of course good staff co-operation is necessary to effect any successful change. It is very much up to you to put your case over well to all your staff in the first place, to be ready to discuss the matter fully and to be able to answer their concerns. Try not to imply that they are 'wrong'; rather that nutrition research is ongoing and that we now know much more about children's health than we used to. Point out, too, that British eating habits have been changing; for example, whereas sweets were once a real treat for children, they have now become routine. Blame the food industry for targeting children with so much worthless and tooth-rotting food, rather than attacking parents or carers. You could say we have all become victims. Let it be known, however, that you do want to implement a given number of the 'healthy eating' changes within a certain period of time.

You should be able to get agreement on at least a few things, and if these are small or gradual changes, such as having fresh fruit more often or sometimes having wholewheat pasta you can implement them right away. I would say there is no need to mention small changes such as these to the children as they will probably not notice them, nor need you mention it when the change simply means more choice, such as when you put out a choice of two kinds of bread instead of only one.

When, however, you stop giving out 'birthday sweets' in favour of stickers, this obviously must be mentioned – and explained – beforehand. A brief word will do: the staff member can say something like 'We're going to have something different for birthdays now. I'm going to make you a special birthday sticker, Jamie. Look, I'm going to draw a face with a lovely big smile just like your smile! If I put it on your jumper you can wear it all day and take it home to show everybody at home. Whereabouts would you like me to put it?' If Jamie mentions the sweet (he may not), the reply could be 'Well, I thought this would be better, really. Sweets rot your teeth, and give you toothache, don't they, so it's a shame. And this will last a lot longer and *everybody* will be able to see it all day and know you're the birthday boy.'

If you have a queuing system to get rid of so the children can help themselves from food in serving bowls on their table, staff could say 'We are going to have a nicer dinner time. Instead of having to queue up and wait about to get your dinner, you can sit down straight away and all the food will be put on the table and you can help yourselves.' It is then important for both food and children to arrive at about the same time!

I think it's a good idea to tell parents when larger changes are envisaged, particularly dietary ones. Inform them all by letter and display a copy on your notice board. Say that in a few weeks time you will be making some changes in the sort of food you are serving in order to fit in with current healthy-eating guidelines. You could say that as sugar causes such damage to children's teeth, there will be fewer foods containing it, no drinks containing sugar (or artificial sweeteners) and no confectionery in the nursery. Point out that there will be more home-cooked food, more fresh fruit, more wholemeal flour and bread and no more salted snacks, such as crisps. Say you hope to widen your repertoire of recipes in order to provide more variety; and that you hope the changes will provide the children with more interesting and enjoyable food as well as a much healthier way of eating. Do encourage parents to discuss the proposed changes with you and your staff, to give their opinion and to ask any questions they may have.

You will probably get great support, although one or two parents with misgivings are inevitably to be expected. With the majority behind you, you can go ahead confidently. However, don't rush it, and give bigger changes (especially) time to settle down before introducing others. Think in terms of months. Always be on the lookout for a better way of doing something.

You might consider having a talk for parents by a local health professional, although evening meetings are difficult for parents without good alternative childcare arrangements. In any case, aim to have a few meetings-cum-social events for parents during the year, perhaps at the end of the day when they collect their children. You could have a spring meeting, perhaps just before Easter, a 'garden party' in the summer, a Bonfire-Night event and another at Christmas. You could give a short talk to parents about any changes that are taking place and how you are keen to provide food that is varied and as nutritious and as enjoyable as possible. Afterwards, all the staff can chat informally with parents and be ready to answer any questions. You could use the occasion to display the sort of foods you are giving the children, and encourage parents to taste. You could put out a special dish for everyone to share – perhaps one which children have helped to prepare. The whole thing should last no longer than about $1\frac{1}{2}$ hours.

6: NURSERY HYGIENE

THIS BOOK CANNOT BE PRECISE about the requirements of any individual nursery. Regulations can change, and can also vary from one local authority to another. It is your responsibility to find out from your authority exactly what the current legal requirements are, and to make sure you are always up to date. Every authority has an Environmental Health department. Its Environmental Health Officers (EHO's) will inspect your premises and can advise you on a range of food safety and hygiene issues. One thing that is required by law is that everyone handling food on your premises (probably the whole staff, as children may be preparing food as an activity) must have a current Basic Food Hygiene Certificate. It is up to you to check your staff's previous training and see that it is updated, usually every three years.

BASIC RULES

That said, there are basic rules of food hygiene that apply anywhere, and you, as manager, are ultimately responsible. You should see that kitchen and care staff – as well as children – observe the basic rules. Never 'leave all that to the cook'. Find a reason to be in the kitchen from time to time and notice how things are done. Sometimes check at the end of the day, especially when you have new staff, that all is in order – the waste bins emptied, milk bottles rinsed and put out, surfaces clear and washed down well, cupboards clean and orderly, tea towels and dish cloths laundered and drying. Look for grime of any kind behind or between fridges, ovens and work tops. Are there any gaps too small to clean? Think how they could be sealed. See if handles or tools feel greasy. There should be no unexplained smell; if there is, investigate it. Even waste bins should have no odour. Check the use-by date on a selection of foods. See if the freezer and fridge need defrosting and check the temperature of both. Is either overfull? Satisfy yourself that the kitchen is impeccable.

The reason for good hygiene is simply to prevent poisoning. Parents trust the nursery to provide clean, safe food. Babies and young children are particularly vulnerable as they have not yet developed resistance to all germs and may become more seriously ill. Severe food poisoning can be fatal.

Poisoning can be the result of poor storage or cooking, but the food can also become contaminated with bacteria from a dirty kitchen or from humans. Meticulous and regular hand washing with warm water and soap is essential during food preparation, particularly after going to the toilet. Failure to do this alone results in much food poisoning in the UK through faecal contamination.

THE MAIN CAUSES OF FOOD POISONING IN THE KITCHEN

- incorrect (usually insufficient) cooking
- keeping cooked food warm too long
- contamination of cooked food by raw food (usually meat and eggs)
- poor personal hygiene

The usual first signs of food poisoning are sickness, diarrhoea and stomach pains. If you suspect a child has food poisoning, act quickly. Contact the parents straightaway and ask them to inform a doctor. Meanwhile, isolate the child as some food poisoning can be contagious. Do not give anything to eat, although plenty of plain water or very diluted fruit juice can be given to prevent dehydration, which can be a potentially serious condition.

SYMPTOMS OF DEHYDRATION

- listlessness
- pinched skin does not spring back normally
- sunken or depressed eyes
- thirst, but not wishing to drink
- dry mouth and tongue
- dry napkin; reduced urine output

If you notice *any* of these, medical help should be sought.

In most cases, children should not return to nursery after a bout of food poisoning until at least 48 hours after all symptoms have ceased and the stools have returned to normal. The child's doctor should advise when to return.

TYPES OF FOOD POISONING BACTERIA

Escherichia Coli (E. coli 0157)
Out of the many types of E. coli organisms, one uncommon type is Verocytotoxin which produces E. coli 0157. It was first noticed in 1982. Children under six years old are especially vulnerable.
Typically found in: raw and under-cooked meats, contaminated beef and beef products, under-processed milk and dairy products and unpasteurised apple juice. It can also be found in yoghurt, cheese, dry-cured salami and even on salad vegetables. It can survive freezing.
Incubation period: 1-6 days.
Symptoms: diarrhoea which can be bloody; it can lead to kidney failure and sometimes death.
To avoid risk: All poultry and all meat products such as mince, sausages, meatballs, burgers should be cooked thoroughly and until no hint of pink remains anywhere in the meat, and juices run clear. Bacteria are destroyed in cooking when the middle of the food reaches 75°C. Frozen meat must be completely thawed before being cooked. Salad vegetables should be washed in running water, including 'ready washed' ones.

Uncooked and ready-to-eat foods must be kept meticulously apart in storage and during preparation to avoid cross-contamination. Keep separate areas and utensils for meat preparation and wash boards and utensils in hot soapy water immediately they have been used, rinse in hot water and put to dry. Work surfaces and hands should also be thoroughly washed, rinsed and dried.

Salmonella

Typically found in: raw and undercooked meat, poultry and eggs; raw, unwashed vegetables; meat pies and pasties; leftover food; unpasteurised milk and dairy products and many other types of food.

Incubation period: 12 -72 hours.

Symptoms: include fever, vomiting, diarrhoea and stomach pains, which may last a week. In rare, severe cases salmonella can be fatal.

To avoid risk: thoroughly thaw frozen meat before cooking; destroy bacteria by heating the food to 70°C for 15 minutes; cook meat and poultry right through; keep ready-to-eat foods separate from uncooked foods to avoid cross-contamination; ensure meticulous personal hygiene.

Campylobacter

This affects four times as many people as salmonella. Less well known than salmonella, perhaps because it's not fatal, and, it is said, because it's a less easy name for journalists to remember!

Typically found in: raw or undercooked meat (especially poultry), excreta (chiefly on meat), untreated water, bird-pecked milk bottles, contamination from pets.

Incubation period: symptoms can take 1-11 days to appear and can last for 2-7 days, and recur over a number of weeks.

Symptoms: there may be a period of fever, with headache and dizziness for a few hours, followed by mild to severe diarrhoea which may be bloody, and severe stomach pains. Most sufferers recover without treatment.

To avoid risk: thaw meat completely before cooking. Thoroughly cook all meat, poultry and unpasteurised milk.

Listeria

Listeria is an environmental organism; one type (only), listeria monocytogenes, may cause illness.

Typically found in: soil, vegetation, raw milk, meat, poultry and salad vegetables and chilled foods such as paté. There is debate over its presence in soft cheeses.

Incubation period: 5-30 days after eating.

Symptoms: various, including mild, flu-like symptoms with fever; blood poisoning (septicaemia) and meningitis; in pregnant women abortion or birth of an infected child; can be fatal especially for babies, very old people and those with weakened immune systems.

To avoid risk: cooking to 75°C and pasteurisation destroys bacteria; unlike other bacteria, listeria bacteria can grow at low temperatures, even in the fridge, so chilled foods such as paté or liver sausage should be used soon after purchase; chilled meals are not recommended for nurseries, but if used must be reheated very well.

Staphylococcus aureus

Typically found in: foods that need handling such as sandwiches, cold desserts, custards and creams; unpasteurised milk. This is because it chiefly comes from human tissues: from cuts and sores on the hands and from coughing or sneezing onto food.

Incubation period: 1-7 hours.

Symptoms: vomiting and stomach cramps; lowered temperature; occasionally diarrhoea; lasts up to 24 hours

To avoid risk: staff with cuts or sores should not handle food; staff must never cough or sneeze near food and all coughs and sneezes must be covered with a handkerchief; staff with colds must not prepare food; avoid dirty equipment; avoid cross-contamination from raw to cooked food; bacteria can be destroyed by heating to 70°C for 15 minutes.

Clostridium botulinum

Typically found in: raw fish; canned food which was not heated enough during canning. It is rare nowadays. Very occasionally it can be found in small amounts in honey, so it is advised that babies under 12 months are not given honey.

Incubation period: 12-36 hours.

Symptoms: double vision; breathing and swallowing difficulties. Death in 1-8 days or slow recovery in 6-8 months.

To avoid risk: avoid damaged or blown cans; don't keep vacuum-packed fish or meat in a warm temperature.

Clostridium perfringens
Typically found in: soil, excreta, meat, poultry, meat dishes, gravies and left-over food.
Incubation period: 8-22 hours.
Symptoms: diarrhoea, stomach pains, nausea, no fever; lasts 12-24 hours.
To avoid risk: avoid contamination with soil; avoid very low temperature cooking in which bacteria can multiply; avoid keeping food warm for a long time or cooling it slowly; ensure good personal hygiene.

Bacillus cereus
Typically found in: incorrectly heated rice dishes; cornflour, meat dishes.
Incubation period: 1-16 hours; lasts up to 24 hours.
Symptoms: nausea, stomach cramps and vomiting within the first 5 hours after eating, or stomach pains and diarrhoea starting 8-16 hours after eating.
To avoid risk: avoid keeping cooked dishes at room temperature or re-heating them for long periods of time. Bacteria can be destroyed by heating to 100°C.

SRSV (small round structured virus)
Typically found in: no food in particular. Strictly speaking they are not food poisoning viruses, but they can be passed from person to person via food.
Incubation period: 1-2 days; the sufferer will be infectious for 48 hours after the symptoms have disappeared.
Symptoms: viral gastroenteritis.
To avoid risk: good general kitchen and personal hygiene. Handwashing between handling different types of food.

HOW TO AVOID FOOD POISONING

The kitchen
Germs can grow quickly in a warm kitchen, so:

• *check that your kitchen fits in with current hygiene rules. If in doubt, ask your local Environmental Health Officer for help.*

- *have fly screens fitted to windows that open. Be determined to keep out all insects, birds and rodents, also any pets – even yours!*

- *line waste bins with plastic bags, and empty at the end of each day – or sooner if the lid won't close. Don't touch the bin with your hands – use the pedal. Periodically, wash out the bin, inside and out.*

- *have separate areas for handling raw food such as meat and fish, and for other foods, each area with its own set of tools, chopping boards and wash cloths. Colour-coding everything helps to keep things separate. Have a dedicated board for raw meat. Wash all tools and surfaces immediately after use. Clean up as you go along.*

- *use a mild disinfectant for wiping surfaces, and disinfect anything that has come into contact with meat.*

- *rinse all boards after use with cold water, then scrub with hot soapy water. Rinse in fresh hot water and put to dry. Don't leave wooden boards (or wooden spoons) in water to soak, or the water will raise the grain of the wood.*

- *make sure **everything** in the kitchen is cleaned regularly – including the wall-mounted tin opener.*

- *keep work surfaces and the draining board very clean all the time and be careful about what you put on them. Stand milk bottles and cartons on paper towels. Wipe the underneath of tins. Never move anything off the floor onto work surfaces.*

- *after cooking, wash **everything** that has been used in hot water and detergent, rinse well in hot water and (preferably) air dry or dry at once with recently sterilised, dry tea towels.*

- *at the end of the day, all dishcloths and tea towels should be boiled and then left to air dry.*

- *mop the floor and dry it after any spills, and mop it all down as the last job each day.*

Care of the fridge

- *1 – 5°C is the correct temperature range – that's as cold as it will go without freezing the food. Keep a thermometer in the fridge on the top shelf near the front, and log the temperature every day. Follow instructions you are given about doing this.*

• *store raw meat (and fish) at the bottom. Nevertheless, put it in trays or bowls which make it impossible for blood to drip onto the shelf.*

• *put cooked food at the top along with dairy produce.*

• *open the door as infrequently as possible. Don't leave the door standing open. The three-seconds limit is ideal to prevent warm air going in and raising the temperature.*

• *put only clean things in the fridge. For example, wipe the underneath of milk bottles and cartons with paper tissue. Wash fruit, vegetables and salads first, or keep them bagged.*

• *don't put hot food into the fridge. Cool it off first; allow no more than $1^{1/2}$ hours for this.*

• *cover all food with plastic, a lid or a plate. It protects it as well as preventing 'refrigerator taste'.*

• *defrost as soon as there is any build up of ice. Do it regularly. Use the opportunity to empty and wash out the fridge with warm water and bicarbonate of soda. Also wash out after any spills. When defrosting, check everything in the fridge for freshness.*

• *keep the fridge reasonably well stocked for fuel efficiency, but not overfull which is not efficient and could mean the fridge is too warm.*

Care of the freezer

• *the temperature must be minus 18°C or lower. Keep a thermometer in it, at the top.*

• *label each food with the date it should be eaten by: look at the manufacturer's recommended storage time: * means one week, ** means one month, *** means three months.*

• *once a food has thawed, it must be either used or, if it is a raw food, cooked and refrozen. If these options are impossible, then throw the food away.*

• *be sure to thaw meat **completely** before cooking it. The safest* way is to thaw it in the bottom of the fridge in order to keep it cold, allowing a day or so for this.

• *frozen vegetables, however, should be cooked from frozen.*

• *defrost the freezer when is has a coating of frost, probably about once a year. When you do this, run the contents down and pack them together in a well-padded container or in the fridge while the freezer defrosts. They should not thaw while this is happening if looked after properly.*

• *go for fresh rather than frozen foods, although it is useful to have a few frozen vegetables such as peas, spinach and sweetcorn, plus some frozen fruit and a reserve of bread, butter and sunflower margarine, some chicken and perhaps some containers of frozen concentrated orange juice.*

Care of cupboards

• *try to position food cupboards where they don't catch the sun. Work out what will be in full sun at 5 a.m. in mid summer – and in a summer evening. If you think there's a problem here, invest in dark blinds to prevent the sun regularly warming up the food in the cupboards. Warm food can soon become infested.*

• *clean, tidy food cupboards are essential. They should be regularly cleaned, and the contents checked for their 'use-by' dates and general condition. Very old food should be discarded. Aim for a not-too-full cupboard: order what you need and use it so everything is as fresh as possible. Flour can become infested with weevils if kept too long.*

• *make sure that fresh vegetables are kept in a cold place. Some should go in the fridge, and the rest need airy but dark storage away from sun and any other heat source. Apples and soft summer fruits should be kept cold, but many fruits such as bananas, pears, plums and tomatoes are often sold under-ripe and may need several days at room temperature to finish ripening.*

Care of the microwave oven

• *Apart from possible staff use, the best advice is not to have a microwave oven, as it is difficult to think how it could be used* *safely for children's food. Babies' bottles should NEVER be heated in a microwave because of the risk of severe burns to the mouth and throat (see page 123). Microwave ovens vary enormously in performance, don't always heat the food to the temperature they say they do, and sometimes cook unevenly, with hot and cold spots. There is thus a danger of dangerously hot food, **and** insufficient cooking with accompanying risk of food poisoning.*

* *Any microwave oven should be kept clean, wiped down from time to time, not forgetting the roof and the hinges.*

Kitchen staff

* *All staff must have a current Food Hygiene Certificate. They must be up to date with current safety regulations. They have a great responsibility of making sure that the children's food is completely safe to eat and must follow good practice. If in doubt over any item of food, they should discard it.*

* *They should be meticulous about personal hygiene. They should wash and re-wash their hands during food preparation between different tasks and after any interruption in work, such as answering the telephone, touching their hair, tying a shoe lace, and particularly after handling waste, coughing, sneezing, using a handkerchief and going to the toilet. It should go without saying that fingernails should be short, unlacquered and perfectly clean.*

* *Staff must wear suitable, protective clothing, including correct shoes, and have their hair tucked under hair nets. All clothing worn must be clean. They must not wear ornate jewellery as it can harbour germs – and may even get lost in the food.*

* *There should be a hand basin in the toilet area as well as one in the kitchen, and, staff should wash their hands twice: once in the toilet area and once again just before handling food or utensils in the kitchen. Hands should be washed with warm water and soap, rubbing the soap over both sides of their hands, between fingers and around fingernails. Hands should then be rinsed in fresh warm water and dried on paper towels or under a hot air drier.*

* *Any cuts, sores or abrasions must be completely covered with*

blue kitchen plasters, and plastic gloves worn as an extra precaution. More serious conditions, along with any infections or bowel trouble must be reported and may require time off work. No one suffering from any type of food poisoning, however mild, should be cooking for others.

- *Staff must never cough or sneeze over food and must cover the mouth with a handkerchief when coughing or sneezing.*

- *There must be first aid provision in the kitchen.*

Cooking

In general, food should not be cooked too far in advance and have to be kept warm. It is recommended that food is cooked until 'piping hot', and if it has to be kept warm, it should be kept at 65°C. As children cannot eat very hot food, staff must avoid serving food that could burn a child's mouth (checking the centre of dishes).

Meat must be kept in the fridge, and frozen meat should be completely thawed (preferably in the fridge) before use.

All meat must be very well cooked right through to the middle. A browned outside does not mean a cooked inside. If meat is undercooked, it will be tough and hard and the children won't be able to eat it anyway.

Meat in casseroles and stews should be cooked until succulent and capable of being cut with a spoon.

Joints of meat are best covered and cooked fairly slowly (170–180°C, gas 3–4) until succulent and easily carved. They should be left to 'rest' for up to half an hour after roasting, covered with a mesh meat cover, to allow the meat to relax and for the juices to set. Minced meat should be cooked until there are no pink bits.

Liver should be cooked very slowly to prevent it becoming hard and dry. It is done immediately the inside has stopped being pink, and should be served quickly. Timing is important if liver is to be enjoyable.

Chicken must be very well done, with the meat almost falling off the bone. A roast chicken is usually done when the legs are loose, but to be sure, a skewer should be inserted into the thickest part (the thigh) to ascertain that the juices run clear, not rosy.

Eggs should be cooked until both yolk and white have hardened. Take care, however, not to cook them so much that they become tough and unpalatable. When the yolks have reached 70°C, they are pasteurised and safe. Boiled eggs should be cooked gently for 7-9 minutes, and then put immediately into a large container of cold water to halt the cooking. Overcooked eggs develop grey-ringed yolks. It is recommended that eggs be stored in the fridge.

Remember not to serve any foods containing raw or lightly cooked eggs such as mousses *unless* you know for sure that the eggs used were pasteurised. Hands should be washed after handling raw eggs.

Green leafy vegetables and salads should be washed well in running water and shaken dry. Pre-packed salads still need washing.

Apples, pears, tomatoes, cucumbers, peppers and items of this sort should be washed in water and ordinary soap before rinsing and using. Because of pesticide use, fruit should be peeled for babies and for very young children. Use a very clean chopping board and knife, especially if food is to be eaten raw. Strawberries should be washed in a sieve under cold running water, then rolled about on absorbant paper until they are dry and shiny, and if not to be eaten soon, put on a covered plate in the fridge. Hull them (pull off their leaves) just before serving to keep the berries fresh.

Raspberries should be rolled about on damp paper to remove any dust. After that, treat as strawberries, above.

Carrots and parsnips should be peeled and then topped and tailed, because of pesticide use, unless they are organic, in which case they need only to be scrubbed well. Use a very clean board and knife, especially if they are to be eaten raw. Peel other vegetables for babies and very young children.

Packets and tins. Buy in small quantities and check the seals are unbroken. Keep in a cool place and discard any that have reached their use-by or best-before date. Use in rotation, using the oldest first. Wipe the lids of tins before opening them. Keep oils in the fridge if there is room; if they warm up too much they will go rancid. Keep flour and rice very cool. When shopping, always read the small print on the label so you know what you are buying.

Clingfilm fastened over food creates a mini 'greenhouse effect' and warms the food up. If you must cover food with clingfilm (as opposed to clean muslin or mesh covers), pierce holes in it to let warm air escape and keep the food cool, preferably in the fridge. Prevent clingfilm touching fatty food.

Leftovers are best avoided at nursery. It sounds wasteful, but leftover cooked food should not be reheated and served again – better safe than sorry. However, if the food can be re-served *cold*, that might be another matter. For example, rice pudding could be served again if it's chilled within $1^{1/2}$ hours and served cold. Leftover potatoes could be made into a salad. But keep such foods no longer than one day and don't mix yesterday's food with today's.

If in doubt: throw away food if it looks, smells or tastes 'off', or if it seems damaged or its texture is unusual, or if you think it may have been contaminated by birds (pecking milk bottle tops, for instance), insects, or animals. Ask your local EHO any questions you may have, or contact The Food Safety Agency Helpline on 0845 7573012. In general: if in doubt, throw it out.

Buying food

Check that food is delivered in suitable containers at an appropriate temperature. Put it away as soon as possible, especially frozen and chilled food. Keep everything out of the sun and away from other sources of heat. When shopping, take cold bags for frozen food and also, in summer, for anything from chiller cabinets. Even so, get the food back to nursery quickly. Keep raw food such as meat, fish and eggs apart from ready-to-eat food. Only use clean shops.

Children and hygiene

Make children aware of basic good hygiene. They should know they must always wash their hands after going to the toilet or touching an animal, and not eat food that has fallen on the floor. Talk about the fact that 'germs can make you ill'.

Mention good hygiene practice when you are shopping or cooking with children. Make sure they wash their hands thoroughly and wear special aprons when they cook. Say that after they have washed their hands, they must not touch their hair or faces again, or anything that's not to do with the food. Talk about why we need good hygiene when you protect something from flies or cough into a handkerchief. Explain, if necessary, why nursery pets must not be allowed near any cooking activity. You could say that animals have germs that are safe for them but are not safe for us.

Safety tips

• *Nuts (or pieces of nuts) should not be given to under fives. Apart from the danger of choking, there are other dangers if a pieces of nut is inhaled.*

• *Any highchairs must be fitted with a safety harness which must be used whenever they are in use.*

• *Children of all ages must be well supervised while they are eating in case they choke or there are other accidents.*

• *The nursery needs to be aware of any food allergies or special diets that children may have (see page 117). It may be safest if nuts and sesame seeds, including peanut butter and tahini, are excluded from the menus (see pages 118-119).*

7: FOOD ACTIVITIES FOR FUN AND EDUCATION

THIS CHAPTER ATTEMPTS only a summary of the large number of enjoyable activities that children can do. Food activities help familiarise children with foods they have not seen or eaten before and can provide opportunities for tasting foods other than at mealtimes. They can also be a way of familiarising parents with foods that the nursery is serving. The obvious food activity is cooking, but there are many others.

Boys and girls should be involved equally in food activities. Also, children should learn that getting ready to prepare food and clearing up afterwards are intrinsic parts of the job which all participants should help with equally to their level of ability.

COOKING WITH CHILDREN

This is usually very popular. Children can either take their food home, or eat it at nursery, perhaps shared with others. Don't just do cake-making, and try to avoid decorating cakes with highly-coloured, sugary bits and pieces. If children make cakes, try to find healthier toppings, perhaps using fresh fruit and curd cheese, but aim to go for less sugary or savoury food such as bread, rolls, fruit buns, fruit bread, banana bread, savoury biscuits, cheese straws, cheese balls, coleslaw, little pizzas with all kinds of toppings – not necessarily with tomato and cheese – and savoury dishes from a variety of different cultures. Parents and staff may be a source of good international recipes.

In addition, children can help to prepare part of their own main meal or a snack. Liaison with kitchen staff is obviously essential, as is having proper tools and a work surface at the right height. Care must be taken that the food preparation area is uncluttered and clean, that the children wear protective clothing which is used only for cooking activities and that basic rules of food hygiene and safety are observed. It may sound ambitious, but under-fives can manage a range of cooking skills including chopping, grating, beating, kneading, and with practice, they soon become proficient. Doing 'real' work for a real meal is reported to boost children's self esteem and even lessen behavioural problems. It also lessens eating problems, as most children find it hard to resist something they have cooked themselves.

Start with small activities, first baking pieces of dough, then making something for a snack, and perhaps then building up to preparing part of a meal. For example, when children are used to play dough, they can move on to making real pastry dough and cheese straws, or on to bread rolls and buns with currants and spice. Bread can be made into various shapes such as teddies, mice, coiled snakes or little cottage loaves.

Children can also chop or break up salad ingredients, or chop vegetables for soup or a stew or stir fry. They can chop up or mash fruit for a dessert. If the dessert consists of plain yoghurt mixed with fruit and orange juice, they could make the whole thing.

Involve children in setting the scene for meal times, laying tables, putting out chairs, clearing away afterwards.

GROWING FOOD PLANTS

Gardening, even indoors, gives children a sense of how food is produced. Growing cress, and sprouting avocado seeds, onions, carrot and beetroot tops and beans are all common nursery activities. Do all of them and more. Have a little 'farm' on the window sill and grow enough cress to cut for tea time. Perhaps do this regularly, planting a crop every week. Try sprouting mung beans and add to a salad or stir fry.

Use your outside area for gardening, too. If you've no earth, most plants can be grown in containers filled with potting compost. Almost any container will do as long as there are drainage holes in the bottom to prevent plants getting waterlogged. Water the plants regularly, which, in summer, means every day it doesn't rain.

Runner beans can be sprouted in jars in the usual way and then carefully planted outside in good soil or in sizeable containers. The plants will need something to climb up, so make a wigwam shape out of long canes tied together, or have the container next to some plastic mesh. Or try dwarf beans that don't need canes. Peas need twiggy sticks or plastic mesh to twine around. When you harvest the beans (or peas), leave one or two pods on the plant to ripen and go brown. Then pick them and show the children the new, big beans and peas inside, just like the ones which were planted – a demonstration of the whole life cycle.

Experiment with plants over the years and see what suits your situation best. Easy plants include potatoes, strawberries, broccoli and spinach (both nicer than bought), and tomatoes, which are an excellent choice, either indoors or out. Try yellow tomatoes too for an attractive display. Try giant sunflowers, sweet smelling, flowering herbs, rocket, raspberries, radishes... If you get a crop, however small, share the children's delight, and enjoy harvesting, sharing and eating it. If there is no crop, remember that the chief aim was to provide an enjoyable and educational experience of growing something from a seed, so still be thrilled at seeing green shoots appear. Being in contact with the soil and living plants is beneficial, and not in every child's experience.

Check that children and staff are covered for tetanus, and that they wash their hands well after gardening.

ART

Various activities here, including making:

• *food pictures. Use stiff card and strong glue and various dry foods such as pasta shapes and pulses, bay leaves, rice, rolled oats, unhulled sunflower seeds and used tea bags. It is usually easier for children to put glue onto the card rather than onto individual items. Perhaps combine with cut out pictures from magazines.*

• *box models. Cover strong boxes with paper and then with items as above; they can then be painted or not.*

• *papier mâché fruit and vegetables, perhaps for sale in a nursery 'shop' or 'café'.*

• *vegetable prints. Use hard vegetables such as halved, small potatoes, carrots or parsnips, or try hard fruits such as apples, using their natural shape.*

• *collages. Children can look in magazines for pictures of food and cut them out. Perhaps ask them to find foods on a given theme such as fish, fruit, vegetables, bread or 'things made from milk'. Sticking the pictures on an appropriately coloured background can make an attractive collage. Staff and parents could be asked to save labels off tins and packets of food.*

FOOD DISPLAYS

Try a display of what you have cooked or grown and invite parents to come and look – and possibly taste – or have a display of foods on a certain theme, such as different types of bread, or raw-and-cooked foods, or food from a certain country, or to celebrate a certain festival. This can make an enjoyable and useful little end-of-day event for the nursery. It may also persuade children to try something on display that is strange to them – especially when they can see all the adults enjoying it.

THE NURSERY SHOP OR CAFÉ

A familiar idea, but from time to time change the type of shop: it could sell groceries, fruit and vegetables, bread and cakes, or be a general store or supermarket and sell everything. Sometimes children could make some real food for sale in the shop or café.

WORDS AND MUSIC

One of the most useful things staff can do is to use the correct *language*. At this age, children's ability to assimilate language is high, and the correct word can almost always be used when talking to children. Staff should use the correct names of foods, utensils and processes and avoid saying something as vague and uneducational as 'pour this into this'.

Much of the mathematical vocabulary that children will learn in infant school can be learned at nursery just by their being used in context. Long words are not necessarily a problem: they can be fun to learn and may be enjoyably repeated. Words such as 'parallel', 'symmetrical', 'angle', 'equal', 'balance' should be used wherever they naturally occur, with simple explanations if necessary, such as 'parallel means that these lines are going the same way as each other all the time. Do you see?'.

One common mistake is to call every straight-sided cooking tin 'square', making it harder for children to understand what exactly a square is later on. Children should not be put in the position of having to unlearn wrongly used words when they go to infant school. It is much harder to *unlearn* something than to learn it in the first place. The names of basic shapes (square, rectangle, triangle, circle) and some three-dimensional shapes (ball, cylinder, cube, pyramid) can be used in many activities, and become familiar. Working with play dough, pastry and bread dough, cutting out biscuits or scones, using baking tins and chopping vegetables can bring in such words.

Similarly, staff should avoid the imprecise use of the word 'bigger' instead of using a more exact word such as 'taller,' 'heavier', 'thicker'. They should also use the word 'smaller' (or 'shorter', 'narrower', 'lighter') to avoid implying that bigger is better.

There are many songs, stories, rhymes and finger plays involving food, which can tie in well with a suitable project. Learn 'One potato, two potato' when planting or harvesting potatoes, for example. Make up relevant new words to tunes the children know, and sing the new song while you cook.

Display some (possibly adult) books with good quality photographs of food, farms, fish, harvests and so on.

MATHEMATICS AND SCIENCE

Cooking offers many opportunities for practical mathematics: counting, sorting, weighing, measuring liquids, experience with one-to-one correspondence, comparison, sequencing and time. Staff should be aware of the possibilities and exploit them, such as letting children sort the vegetables for making soup, instead of putting them out ready sorted. If a procedure is too difficult for children to do, they could at least watch it being done, with accompanying explanation.

Laying the dinner table with one plate for everyone and so on teaches one-to-one correspondence, while counting, using both cardinal and ordinal numbers, can be built into a host of activities. Staff should encourage children's sense of curiosity by asking such questions as 'Guess how many buns like this we can make out of this mixture,' and 'What do you think will happen if...?' Note their answers and then find out together. Asking children how they think their world functions can produce insight into their thinking and give ideas for further activities.

Try little 'experiments' involving volume and capacity, gravity, freezing and melting, solubility, absorbency and the effects of sunlight on plants. Growing plants and cooking provide a wealth of ideas, and can also involve measuring and recording. Try a project on fruit, or on bread, fish, farms or on milk. Involve art, music, drama, stories, language work, as well as mathematics and science. Keep all projects rich in language and accurate in vocabulary.

OUTINGS

Outings provide rich experiences. A walk to a local market stall or specialist food shop can further widen children's horizons. Children can go with staff regularly to buy food for the nursery. Perhaps arrange visits to some local allotments or kitchen garden, a working windmill, a cultural centre or city farm.

FEEDING BIRDS AND ANIMALS

Feed the birds in winter (only), feed the nursery pets, and talk about what different creatures like to eat.

8: MATTERS FOR CONSIDERATION

THESE ARE SOME OF THE MATTERS which a nursery needs to know about and act upon, and which parents may ask about.

MULTICULTURAL PROVISION

The nursery has a duty to treat each child as an individual, and this applies to food as much as anything else. Menus should reflect the cultural and religious background of all the nursery's children – as should food activities, including the home corner and displays. In menu planning, it must be remembered that avoidance of certain foods is crucial in some cultures. Following very strict dietary laws may be impossible for a small nursery kitchen, but every nursery can manage food avoidances. Offering vegetarian food can be an easy solution.

In addition to having correct ingredients, the food should be prepared and served in the appropriate way so that it looks and tastes familiar. In addition, children should be able to eat their food in the way their culture requires. If the nursery is unsure about any aspect of food preparation then the parents or other carers should be consulted.

Food customs vary from one community to another, and families can interpret the general rules differently. Some families are strict within the home but less so, elsewhere. The nursery should discuss this with each child's parents. Interviews with new parents provide an ideal opportunity. Traditional foods tend to be healthy, and generally speaking, menu planners should know more about their nutritional value. Parents and other carers can be a good source of recipes and information on how to cook and present food. Perhaps a parent could come and demonstrate something?

Serving special occasion food for festivals and on religious occasions can be a good way for a nursery to celebrate the cultural diversity of its children as well as being a way of involving parents. Again, parents could be a good source of information. The nursery might wish to accept offers of food from parents for a special day, in which case, the nursery needs to plan carefully and consult with parents. Try to have a variety of foods so the children have a choice. The mix of children in the group will largely determine which occasions to celebrate, but whatever the mix, the nursery should celebrate a range of cultural events.

DIETARY CUSTOMS

	Jewish	Sikh	Muslim	Hindu	Buddhist	Rastafarian *
Eggs	No blood spots	Yes	Some	Yes	Some	Usually
Milk, yoghurt	Not with meat	Yes	Yes	Yes	Yes	Usually
Cheese	Not with meat	Some	Some	Some	Yes	Usually
Butter, ghee	Kosher	Some	Some	Some	No	Some
Lard	No	No	No	No	No	No
Chicken	Kosher	Yes	Halal	Some	No	Some
Lamb	Kosher	Yes	Some	Halal	No	Some
Beef	Kosher	No	Halal	No	No	Some
Pork, ham, bacon	No	Rarely	No	No	No	No
Fish	With fins and scales	Some	No	Some	Some	Some
Shellfish	No	Some	Some	Some	No	No

Cereal foods, fruits, vegetables, peas, beans and lentils are eaten by all these groups.
* some Rastafarians are vegan

INTERNATIONAL FESTIVALS AND CELEBRATIONS	
1 January 6 January 7 January 25 January	New Year Epiphany: 3 Kings Day Rastafarian New Year Burns Night
Late January, early February	Chinese New Year • Japanese New Year for Trees
3 February	Japanese bean-scattering ceremony
40 days before Easter	Shrove Tuesday (pancake day) • Mardi Gras
Late February, early March	Latin American and Caribbean Carnival • Ching Ming, Chinese festival of light • Purim (Jewish)
17 March 21 March	St. Patrick's Day Baha'I New Year • Holi (Hindu harvest festival)
Three weeks before Easter	Mothering Sunday
March/April	Passover (Jewish festival of Pesach) • Easter
1 May	May Day • Wesak (Buddhist festival on the first full moon in May)
Late May/June	Shavout (Jewish festival of weeks) • Tuan Yang Chieh (Chinese dragon boat festival)
c.15 June	Obon, Japanese festival
August	Raksha Bhandhan (Indian festival of brotherly & sisterly love)
September/October	Yom Kippur (Jewish New Year) • Chinese kite festival • Harvest festival
31 October	Hallowe'en
October/November	Dussehra (10 day Hindu celebration) • Diwali (Hindu festival of light)
5 November 15 November	Guy Fawkes (bonfire night) Shichi-go-san (Japanese festival for boys of 5 and girls of 3 and 7)
Last Thursday in November	(USA and Canadian Thanksgiving Day)
December	Hannukah (Jewish festival)
25 December 26 December	Christmas Day Boxing day
Moveable feasts	Ramadan, the Muslim month of fasting moves roughly ten days earlier each year. Children under 13 are not usually expected to fast. The fasting month ends with the festival of Eid-al-Fitr. Check these dates with parents, or contact SHAP (see page 134).

SPECIAL DIETS

It is the nursery's duty to provide special diets when children need them. A child may have a medical condition requiring a special diet, and some parents may wish their children to have vegetarian food. It is the parents' responsibility to inform the nursery about this, but the nursery should always ask, and consult with a child's parents or carers about the diet. Sometimes, a parent may wish to bring food in, especially with a very strict diet. The nursery should also seek advice from a State Registered Dietitian.

Vegetarian diets

Vegetarians eat 'no fish, flesh or fowl'. However, some vegetarians eat fish or chicken, so the nursery must ascertain how the word 'vegetarian' is being interpreted.

Eggs, milk, cheese and yoghurt are all good alternatives to meat and fish protein. In addition, soya 'meat', Qorn and tofu (beancurd) can be incorporated into delicious recipes and be much liked by children. Good protein can also be made by eating a grain food (bread, buns, rice, pasta, oats, semolina, sweetcorn) and pulses (peas, beans, lentils, chickpeas) *in the same meal*. Beans on toast is an example of 'complementary' or 'incomplete' proteins combining to make a protein-rich meal.

Iron in vegetarian diets

First please read pages 21-23 on iron.

Without red meat, it is more difficult to ensure that children get sufficient iron. The best sources are oily fish (if the child eats fish) such as sardines and pilchards, plus eggs, pulses, wholewheat bread, wheat germ (such as Bemax), broccoli, dried fruit, and some fortified breakfast cereals. Having a vitamin C-rich food or drink at mealtimes will aid iron absorption. Vitamin drops contain iron and are suitable for vegetarians.

If the nursery builds a variety of dairy foods, cereals, pulses, dried and fresh fruit, vegetables and eggs into its vegetarian menus then sufficient nutrients should be supplied. Tea and coffee should be avoided at mealtimes as they prevent iron being absorbed.

Vegan diets

Vegans can obtain protein by combining 'complementary' proteins in the way described above, but without any animal food at all there is no natural source of vitamin B12. However, it is added to some commercial foods. It is probable that any vegan parents will offer to bring in suitable food. Otherwise, the nursery should consult both with the parents and with a State Registered Dietitian.

FOOD ALLERGY AND INTOLERANCE

PEANUT ALLERGY

Peanuts in any form are dangerous to an allergic child who can rapidly be made very ill by merely being in the same room as others who are eating peanuts, or by touching them afterwards. Facial swelling and breathing difficulties are two symptoms, and urgent medical treatment in hospital is essential. It could be safest for the nursery to avoid all forms of peanuts completely, and it certainly must do so if any child has this allergy. It is best not to give any type of nuts (or sesame seed products) to babies under six months, nor to children under three years old with a family history of allergy.

Look out for labels which say 'may contain nuts', and also for the words nuts, groundnuts, monkey nuts, earthnuts, peanut butter, peanut oil, groundnut oil, arachis oil, arachis hypogaea, nut butter, nut paste, marzipan, frangipane, praline, goober, goober peas, pinder, hydrolysed vegetable oils and protein, and additives such as nut extract, nut flavour, lecithin, E471 and E472. Lipsticks may contain peanut oil.

Unfortunately, food labels don't always list small amounts. A State Registered Dietitian should be consulted over planning diets for allergic children. Periodically checking with manufacturers is wise as formulations can change.

Medically provable allergies affect less than two people in a hundred, although many more than that claim to be allergic. The nursery should check with parents that any intolerance or allergy has been medically ascertained. It is unwise to restrict a child's diet without advice from a doctor or State Registered Dietitian. Dislike of a food, unpleasant associations or food battles with parents are some of the reasons for a child being labelled allergic.

However, in genuine cases, people can be made seriously ill by consuming something they are allergic to. Peanuts, peanut butter, sesame seeds, sesame butter (tahini), nuts, cows' milk, eggs, citrus fruit, soya beans, wheat and other cereals, strawberries, fish and shellfish are some of the most common allergens. A few children react badly to certain additives (see page 41).

Coeliac disease (allergy to grains except rye, maize and rice), **lactose intolerance** (inability to digest lactose, the sugar in milk), **milk protein allergy, diabetes** (problems in dealing with sugars), **cerebral palsy** (possible chewing and swallowing difficulties) and **cystic fibrosis** (enzymes which digest food cannot function because of blocked pancreatic ducts) all require special diets which should be within the nursery's scope. Professional advice and parental consultation are essential.

CONCERN OVER FATNESS IN CHILDREN

If parents express concern of an overweight child, the general advice should be that the child should be given more opportunity for daily, energetic exercise. Removing between-meal snacks, particularly soft drinks, confectionery and salted snacks, and thus removing a massive source of high-calorie but low-nutrient foods, is also desirable.

A good, sugar-free breakfast (see page 65) should be recommended, as well as other nutritionally sound meals. The child should not be given some kind of 'low-calorie' diet, of the sort recommended for adult slimmers. If this regimen appears not to work after several weeks, the parents should seek advice from the child's GP, who may refer them to a State Registered Dietitian.

ORGANIC FOOD

'Organic' is a legally protected term. All organic food production is governed by a strict set of rules. Anything carrying the symbol of the Soil Association, or of a few other registered certification bodies, has been inspected and certified as genuinely organic. The Soil Association says 'Organic agriculture avoids the use of chemical pesticides and fertilizers, relying instead on developing a healthy, fertile soil and growing a mixture of crops. Farms can stay biologically balanced with a wide variety of beneficial insects and other wildlife to act as natural predators for crop pests, and a soil full of micro-organisms and earthworms to maintain its vitality.

'Animals are reared without the use of antibiotics, drugs and wormers. They have access to fields and are allowed to express their natural behaviour patterns. They have comfortable bedding and plenty of indoor space. Wherever possible, they are given natural, organic feedstuffs.'

Organic food from abroad should be similarly certified. All organic food is free from genetically modified organisms, and the Soil Association says that there has been no recorded case of BSE on farms that have been managed organically since 1985. It has tight regulations to keep BSE out of organic herds.

There is no question that organic farming is better for the environment. Figures on the removal of hedgerows, loss of trees, ponds and wildlife of all kinds are stupendous and still rising. We have lost 50% of our ancient woodlands since the last war, and thousands upon thousands of miles of hedgerows. Chemical fertilizers, pesticides, herbicides, fungicides and so on wash off the land into rivers, ponds and into our water supply, even into deep borehole water. Apple and pear trees, for example, are sprayed over 30 times with agrochemicals every season. The routine use of antibiotics in farm animals kept in 'intensive' conditions has contributed to human over consumption. Children are particularly at risk from chemical residues because of their small body size: the smaller the child, the greater the risk.

Many parents are keen for their young children to consume food that is pesticide-free, and some nurseries have made it their aim – and selling point – to provide as much organic food as possible. At any rate, all nurseries should:

• *top, tail and peel all non-organic carrots and parsnips and other root vegetables as these absorb the most chemicals. Wash other produce well.*

• *peel non-organic apples and pears at least for babies and younger children.*

• *discard the outer leaves of lettuces and green leafy vegetables, which will have absorbed the most spray.*

• *go for organic produce whenever possible. Contact local growers. Contact local shops for bargain buys of produce that has reached its display-by date. Bananas can still be green by then!*

• *BUT, continue to serve plenty of fruits, vegetables and milk and cereal foods. The nutritional benefits of these very nutritious foods far outweigh the disadvantages of any chemical residues and help fight off any ill-effects. (See pages 33 and 34 for sources of further information.)*

GENETICALLY MODIFIED FOOD

This is a highly contentious issue surrounded by much concern and uncertainty. The nursery should be able to avoid GM foods by means of a little research, and more and more manufacturers and supermarkets are removing GM ingredients from sale. The book *GM Free: a shopper's guide to genetically modified food* (see page 132) should assist you.

9: AND WHAT ABOUT BABIES?

NURSERIES ARE TAKING IN MORE BABIES than they used to, so this aspect deserves a particular mention. It is especially important here for the nursery to be in close contact with mothers and not to disrupt feeding patterns established at home.

MILK

Breastfeeding

Breast milk is universally acknowledged to be best. For the first four to six months of a baby's life this living fluid is a complete and perfect food, and it changes over time as the baby grows. It contains antibodies which fight infections, it passes on some of the mother's immunities and reduces the risks of allergic reactions. It may help prevent certain diseases such as heart disease and diabetes in later life. It can be a baby's main drink for the whole of the first year. Before four months of age, no other food or drink, not even boiled water, should be given to a baby who is being breastfed.

If a mother is still breastfeeding, the nursery should do what it can to enable her to continue. A working mother should feel welcome to breastfeed her baby at the nursery if she wishes, and the nursery should provide her with a private, warm room for this. Expressed milk can be left at nursery each day and at the end of the day any leftover milk should be returned to the parent.

Infant formula

This is usually made from cows' milk which has been modified for humans. There are two types, one with more casein (the protein in milk) or one with more whey. It is thought that 'whey dominant' formulas are more like breast milk and therefore more suitable for (at least) young babies. Both types appear to meet babies' nutritional needs, but of course do not have the additional benefits of human milk.

BOTTLE FEEDING

• Babies should be fed by the same member of staff each time in order to foster a warm relationship. The baby should be held closely throughout the feed. The carer should make regular eye contact with the baby and from time to time should smile, talk or sing softly to the baby. The feeding time should be relaxed, unhurried, and an enjoyable experience for the baby.

• Babies must never be left alone while they are feeding or be propped up with their bottles. It is dangerous and inappropriate for their emotional needs.

• Parents should be encouraged to make up the feeds for their own children, with each bottle clearly labelled with the name of the child and the date and time the feed was made. The nursery should refrigerate the bottles. Any leftover milk should be returned to the parent at the end of each day.

• If the nursery makes up the feeds, it is preferable to have a dedicated area for doing this and strict hygiene must be observed. All equipment must be sterilised before use. All bottles and teats must be thoroughly cleaned and must also be sterilised for babies under six months. Freshly-boiled tap water should be used, never bottled or sterilised water. Manufacturers' instructions for making the feed should be followed precisely.

• Microwaves should NEVER be used to heat babies' bottles. Severe burns have been caused to babies' mouths and throats by this practice, as the milk can become very hot while the bottle remains cool. Bottle warmers are ideal.

• Nothing except milk should ever be put into babies' bottles.

Infant formula milks are usually the only recommended alternative to breast milk and can be used for the whole of the first year as a main drink. If formula milk is given, the nursery should normally continue with the same one that the baby is used to.

'Follow-on' milks

Sold as suitable for older babies, although there is no evidence that they have any developmental or growth advantages for babies who eat a normal, good mixed diet.

Soy milk: Use only calcium-enriched brands, but soy milks must not be given to babies without definite medical advice. There are also concerns that oestrogen-like substances in soy milk can adversely affect a baby's development. (Some chronic infant constipation can be cured by substituting soy milk for cows' milk, but this is a medical decision.)

Cows' milk: This is not suitable as a main drink for babies under one year old.

WEANING

Weaning is the gradual change from an all-milk diet to a mixed-food diet ('solids'). It should begin no earlier than four months as a baby's digestive system is too undeveloped to cope with food before then. By six months the baby should be enjoying some 'solids', and by one year, should be eating three good meals a day plus two or three healthy snacks.

New foods should be introduced one at a time. If a food is rejected it should be removed and offered again a week or so later. The repertoire of foods should gradually expand so that by the age of one year, babies are enjoying a wide variety of foods. Similarly, the texture of the food should gradually change from being puréed to mashed, and then to finely chopped or minced, in line with developing chewing skills.

The National Children's Bureau recommends that *"Parents should always be consulted about when they wish solids to be introduced and which solids to provide. Parents may wish to provide their own weaning foods... and it is recommended that the nursery does not disrupt patterns established at home"*. Staff should remember that each baby eats at its own pace, and this should be respected, so the meal is relaxed and enjoyable. Babies should be allowed and encouraged to feed themselves when they are able.

WEANING PLAN

Do not give salt, sugar, any kind of artificial sweeteners, nuts (or nut butters or nut oils), 'hot' spices, very fatty food or bottled drinks, tea or coffee at any stage of weaning.

The first stage, 4-6 months
  Suitable first foods:
• baby rice prepared with breast or formula milk, and vegetables and fruit such as potatoes, carrots, apples and pears, all peeled, cooked and puréed. At first these can be just a taste, sucked off a carer's finger, and then taken from the tip of a small plastic spoon.
• other puréed vegetables and fruit can be added gradually, such as puréed soft-cooked peas and lentils and very tender meat and fish.
  Do not give:
• wheat in any form (bread, biscuits, pasta, semolina, etc.) or oatmeal, to avoid triggering an allergy (coeliac disease) • eggs • citrus fruits or juices or soft summer fruits • spinach, beetroot, turnip, swede • cows' milk or milk products

Second stage, 6-8 months
  You can add:
• well-cooked egg yolk (but not the white yet) • soft-cooked beans • wheat-based food and oats • ripe banana, avocado, citrus and summer fruits • spinach, swede, turnip
  Do not give:
• egg whites

Third stage, 9-12 months
You can add:
• well-cooked egg white • oily fish
  Do not give:
• cows' milk except as plain yoghurt, cheese, or to mix with food

If commercial 'baby foods' are given, the manufacturer's instructions should be followed and any uneaten food thrown away. Such foods should not be used in quantity as they tend to be bland and too predictable in taste and texture. They usually do not taste like home cooked food and thus tend to prepare babies' palates for the flavours of mass-produced commercial foods rather than families' own cooking.

Points to remember

• *After four months of age, the stores of iron that babies were born with are becoming exhausted and need replenishing. Animal sources of iron are absorbed best. Liver (give no more than once a week), kidney and red meat are iron-rich foods which can be puréed or mashed. Mashed beans, peas, lentils, and dried fruit are also good sources. After nine months, sardines, pilchards and tuna can be given.*

• *Give food on a spoon, but when the baby is able to hold food, offer finger foods too. Try pieces of soft fruit, semi-cooked pieces of vegetable, flakes of fish and pieces of succulent meat from a casserole. Later, rice crackers, pieces of different kinds of cheese, plain bread sticks, bread and toast fingers will give experience of different textures.*

• *It is recommended that babies under the age of one year should be given vitamin drops (containing vitamins A, C and D). Health visitors or GP's can advise families.*

• *Non-organic carrots and parsnips should be topped, tailed and peeled first. Non-organic potatoes, apples and pears should be peeled for babies.*

• *Unpasteurised milk, yoghurt and cheese should not be given to babies.*

• *Children must not be left alone while they are eating, in case they choke.*

• *. Only milk (breast or formula) should be put into babies' bottles. It is particularly damaging for sweet drinks, including diluted fruit juices, to be put into bottles because the sugar and acid in the drink will have a long time to wash around the gums and newly emerging teeth. This causes what has become known as* *'bottle caries': when new teeth are black and decayed. Sometimes new teeth erupt already decayed.*

• Food must never be put into babies' bottles. It could cause choking and doesn't teach a baby that different foods must be handled differently in the mouth.

• After the age of six months, gently encourage babies to drink from a beaker or cup.

• Babies should be weaned off their bottles by the age of one year.

• Breast milk, formula milk and plain water are the only drinks a baby need be offered. Very diluted fresh fruit juice (diluted with water 1:8) can be given at mealtimes to aid the absorption of iron, but not at other times because of risks to teeth. Such drinks can easily establish a preference for sweet-tasting drinks, causing children to reject drinks which don't taste sweet. Tea and coffee, bottled water, 'diet' drinks, squash, soft drinks and ready-made commercial drinks of all kinds are all unsuitable. They either rot teeth, or contain caffeine which inhibits iron absorption, or are too high in minerals for babies. Commercial 'baby' and 'baby herbal' drinks have no benefits for babies.

• Children should be encouraged to feed themselves as soon as they are able, however messy it may be. By the age of two, many children are able to help themselves from serving bowls.

10: WHERE TO FIND MORE HELP?

THIS CHAPTER LISTS PEOPLE, organisations, books and reports which a nursery manager could look to for further help.

PEOPLE ON YOUR DOORSTEP

If you are trying to find an orchard to visit, or an authentic recipe, or a butcher who will make you some lean, low-salt sausages, start with your staff and parents. Put up a notice and ask likely people personally. There may be a wealth of local knowledge and skills there just waiting to be discovered! Be very appreciative of suggestions, and when accepting offers of practical help, make sure no one feels 'used'. Paying parents something for actual work, such as planting a nursery apple tree, or sewing aprons or putting up batons and hooks in a cookery area, helps prevent ill feeling afterwards – it can easily happen.

Also, talk to other local nurseries, and people you meet on courses. How did they find their wonderful cook? How do they organise snacks? Try to arrange 'food workshops' with other nurseries to exchange recipes and pool experiences.

FURTHER AFIELD

Local libraries, shops, markets

Use them for regular local trips. For example, a staff member could visit the local fishmonger each week, taking a different quartet of children each time. Such visits can be very educational. Perhaps invite someone from a local shop or restaurant into the nursery to show something of what they do. Libraries offer a free service and can be extremely helpful with information for food activities. Some loan pictures and other items.

Use small shops wherever you can, although walking round a supermarket with children can provide insight into their eating habits at home. Also, it's easy to inspect and discuss the various products on sale there, and do a bit of consumer education. For example, have a look at the labels with the children to see if there is a lot of added sugar ('toothache food') and how much real fruit a product has ('or is it just pretending?'), and so on. You could discuss how much the picture on the packet tells you about the food. Is what's pictured on the box the same thing as the food inside? Why is that kind of picture there? You may get some interesting replies.

Religious and cultural centres
A visit to any of these can also be very educational, especially when related to a festival. Ask if a visit would be welcome.

Environmental health officers
These people work for the local council's Environmental Health department. They will inspect your premises and can advise you about hygiene and food safety. Contact them quickly if you doubt the safety of any food, or if several children show symptoms of 'tummy bugs' such as sickness or diarrhoea.

Community dietitians and health promotion officers
Based at the Dietetics department of district hospitals, they advise on healthy eating in the community. They could offer posters and leaflets and help with improving your menus and with special diets. They might be willing to give a talk to parents.

Health promotion officers
Contact them at your local authority's Health Promotion Unit (or, in Scotland, your local health board or Health Education Board) for general health promotion matters, including training

for staff. They too might be willing to talk to parents. They can supply Health Education Authority publications, perhaps free.

Community dental officers

As above, but for healthy eating as it affects teeth. Some do presentations for children as well as for parents.

Primary resource co-ordinators

Some local authorities have full-time officers for under fives. At any rate, there should be an 'Early Years' department. See what materials and support they offer.

Companies, trade associations

It is no secret that some are very keen to get into nurseries and schools in order to promote their products to a captive audience. It may be best to avoid them completely. On the other hand, companies often have useful posters and leaflets. If you use these, be meticulous about masking the product names and logos. If this is impossible with a product, don't use it, as even subtle selling messages can be insidious, and if parents complain you won't have a leg to stand on.

FURTHER READING

Birth to Five: A Complete Guide to the First Five Years of Being a Parent. Free to all new parents through Health Promotion Units.

Child Development form Birth to Eight: a Practical Focus, The National Children's Bureau, London, tel: 020 7843 6000.

Children's Food, and *Reading Food Labels* and *GM Food.* 3 posters available from The Food Commission (see listing). £2.50 each inc p&p.

Children's Food Examined: an analysis of 358 products targeted at children, Dr Karla Fitzhugh and Dr. Tim Lobstein. The Food Commission (see listing) (2000). Price £20. It details the high amount of sugar, salt and fat in nearly all the foods marketed directly at children. Summary in issue 49 of The Food Magazine (see listing).

Department of Health Publications, PO Box 410, Wetherby LS23 7LN, tel: 01937-840250 Various publications, including the booklet *Breastfeeding: Good Practice Guidance to the NHS,* the leaflet *Welfare Milk and Vitamins: A Guide for Families,* and the leaflet and poster *What's for Dinner Today Mum? A Short Guide to Weaning.*

Easy to Swallow, Hard to Stomach: the results of a survey of food advertising on television, Sue Dibb and Andrea Castell. The National Food Alliance (now Sustain, see listing) (1995).

Eating Well for Under 5's in Child Care, The Caroline Walker Trust (1998). A detailed and comprehensive report with many recommendations by an Expert Working Group for carers of young children, which aims to help re-establish good food as the basis of good health. Copies available from: CWT, 22 Kindersley Way, Abbotts Langley WD5 0DQ (Cheques payable to The Caroline Walker Trust).

Festival Booklets Set, NES Arnold, tel: 0115 945 2201

Festivals and Celebrations, Jim Fitzsimmons & Rhona Whiteford. Scholastic Educational Books (1994).

Folate - Mass Fortification for All?, Food Magazine no. 52. January 2001. Available from The Food Commission (see listing). Price, £3.50 inc p & p.

The Food Magazine, The Food Commission (see listing). The magazine reports on food issues such as commercial baby foods, food advertising and labelling, BSE, food irradiation, genetic engineering etc. and is an excellent way of keeping up to date on food issues. £19.50 per year. The Food Commission is an independent watchdog on food, and sells various books and reports.

Fortification Examined: How nutrients can undermine good nutrition, Gillie Bonner, (State Registered Dietitian), Hugh Warwick, Martin Barnado & Tim Lobstein. Available from the

Food Commission (see listing). 100-page report surveying 260 food products with added vitamins and minerals. Price £20. Summary in issue 46 of The Food Magazine (see listing).

GM Free: A Shopper's Guide to Genetically Modified Food, Sue Dibb & Tim Lobstein. Thorsons (1999). An explanation of the issues, what is known and what is not, and how to make food choices.

Good for Sales, Bad for Babies, article in *The Food Magazine* from the Food Commission (see listing), issue 48, January 2000. A survey of the amounts of sugar added to various baby food products.

Health Education Authority Publications: HEA Customer Services, Marston Book Services, PO Box 269, Abingdon, Oxon OX14 4YN, tel: 01235-465565: The leaflets *Breastfeeding Your Baby* and *Weaning Your Baby,* and the booklets *Keeping Baby Teeth Healthy: Tooth Care for 0-2 Year Olds, Caring For Your Children's Teeth: A Guide for 3-11 Year Olds,* and *If You Worship The Sun Don't Sacrifice Your Skin: How To Protect Your Skin From Sun Damage.*

Healthy Eating for Babies and Children, Mary Whiting & Tim Lobstein. Hodder & Stoughton (1995). A guide for parents from conception to schooldays. Over 60 pages of recipes.

Ministry of Agriculture, Fisheries and Food (MAFF) Publications: Foodsense, Admail 6000, London SW1 2XX, tel: 0645-556000: Various free booklets, including: *Keeping Food Cool and Safe, Food Allergy and Other Unpleasant reactions to Food, Food Safety, Ten Tips for Food Safety* (and also posters in A2, A4 and A5), *The Food Safety Act 1990 and You* (a summary of the Act), and *Be Allergy Aware,* containing advice for catering establishments.

National Diet and Nutrition Survey: Children aged 1½ - 4½ Years, Volume One, Clarke PC, Collins DL, Davies PSW, Gregory JR & Hughes JM. HMSO, London (1995) Report of Diet and Nutrition Survey.

The Nursery Food Book, 2nd Edition, Mary Whiting & Tim Lobstein. Arnold (1998)
A comprehensive and highly practical book which combines the theory of good nutrition with the day to day practice of childcare. Written for all nursery workers and students, and used in many colleges. Full of ideas for food activities, including gardening and basic skills. Over 50 recipes, plus ideas for sandwiches and snacks.

Nursery World Magazine, TSL Education Ltd. Weekly magazine for child carers covering a wide range of topics.

School Meals: first report by the Education and Employment Committee, House of Commons Session 1999-2000. HMSO (2000).

The Shopper's Guide to Organic Food, Lynda Brown. Fourth Estate (1998)
All you need to know about organic food and farming, with an A-Z guide to organic foods.

Weaning and the Weaning Diet, COMA Report. HMSO (1994).

Young Children in Group Daycare: Guideline for Good Practice, National Children's Bureau (see listing).

USEFUL CONTACTS

Anaphylaxis Campaign
PO Box 149
Fleet
Hampshire GU13 0FA
tel: 01252-542-029

British Allergy Foundation
Deepdene House
30 Bellegrove Road
Welling
Kent DA16 3BY
tel: 020-8303-8525

Diabetes UK
10 Queen Anne Street
London W1M 0BD
tel: 020-7323-1531

British Dietetic Association (Paediatric Group)
7th floor, Elizabeth House
22 Suffolk Street
Queensway
Birmingham B1 1LS
tel: 0121-616-5490

Coeliac Society
PO Box 220
High Wycombe
Bucks HP11 2HY
tel: 01494-437-278

Community Practitioners' and Health Visitors'
Association
40 Bermondsey Street
London SE1 3UD
tel: 020-7717-4000

Food Commission
94 White Lion Street
London N1 9PF
tel: 020-7837-2250

Health Education Authority
30 Great Peter Street
London SW1P 2HW
Tel: 020-7222-5300

Hyperactive Children's Support Group
71 Whyke Lane
Chichester PO19 2LD
tel: 01903-725-182

National Asthma Campaign
Providence House
Providence Place
London N1 0NT
tel: 020-7226-2260

National Children's Bureau
Early Childhood Unit
8 Wakley Street
London EC14 7QE
Tel: 020-7843-6000

Parents at Work
45 Beech Street
London EC2Y 8AD
tel: 020-7628-3565

Pesticides Action Network *UK*
Eurolink Business Centre
49 Effra Road
London SW2 1BZ
tel: 020-7274-8895

SHAP Working Party
c/o National Society Religious Education Centre
36 Causton Street
London SW1P 4AU
tel: 020-7932-1194

Sustain
94 White Lion Street
London N1 9PF
tel: 020-7837-1228

Soil Association
40-56 Victoria Street
Bristol BS1 6BY
tel: 0117-929-0661

Vegetarian Society
Parkdale
Dunham Road
Altrincham
Cheshire WA14 4QG
tel: 0161-928-0793

INDEX